ALWAYS NEVER FOREVER

Six Narrative Monologues

Skip Pulley

Catharsis Publishing

Always Never Forever
Second Edition

ISBN-13: 978-0692732564
ISBN-10: 069273256X

2014 Catharsis Publishing
A Literary Cooperative

Always Never Forever

Skip Pulley

Contents

The mass of men lead lives of quiet desperation
Henry David Thoreau

Preface

Most writers do not *become* writers, they simply realize one day that they *are* writers. I realized this in 1989, at age 16. My writing career began as a freelance contributor. I wrote live music reviews and creative nonfiction, mostly narrative essays. At the time, all my literary idols were transcendentalists. I admired many of the authors personally and I loved their writing style. Transcendentalism validated my belief system and reassured me that a purpose for all life existed. Through study and observation I learned that the human "self" is invariably linked to nature. I learned that social institutions such as organized religion and the political process ultimately corrupt the individual. Human beings are designed to be self-reliant and autonomous, thereby able to form true community. Like most philosophical movements, transcendentalism is a big word that describes a simple idea. Humans have knowledge about themselves and their universe that transcends or goes beyond the 5 senses (what we can see, hear, taste, touch and feel). In other words, "matter" is not all that matters.

Transcendentalists were outspoken critics of unconscious conformity in contemporary society. Ralph Waldo Emerson said it best, as he urged everyone to "enjoy an original relation to the universe". My favorite transcendental authors are Henry David Thoreau, Nathaniel Hawthorne, Walt Whitman and Herman Melville. As a young writer, I wanted to someday number among them. But at age 16, I was insolent. I was intelligent, but I was also inexperienced and slightly naïve. Like most young writers I had more questions than answers. I was restless and eager to be published. I wanted to make a permanent impression of words on paper. I considered myself a naturalist, but my editors classified me as postmodern. Eventually, I realized my style was existential. So in addition to literary realism, which I used to describe how society, heredity and environment influenced human behavior, I also began to study existential philosophy.

Philosophers such as Søren Kierkegaard and Friedrich Nietzsche laid the groundwork for the intellectual movement known as existentialism in the mid-19th century, by dismantling objectivity and embracing skepticism of social norms. Based on their conclusions, my belief is that subjectivity is the path to objective truth and vice versa – the nexus of which forms a "composite" truth. The first step on this path is an understanding of the distinction. I feel that the line between objective and subjective truth has been intentionally obscured by an overall displacement of the archetype by later generations of existential philosophers. As a result, writers such as Jean-Paul Sartre, Albert Camus and Samuel Beckett drew heavily from Kierkegaard and Nietzsche rather than their contemporaries. These post-war existentialists brought a new sense of subjectivity, but also a sense of hopelessness which greatly influenced thinkers, writers and artists of that era.

For example, Karl Barth's fideist approach to theology and lifestyle ironically spawned irreverence for reason and sparked the rise of subjectivity. Post World War II colonialism greatly contributed to the idea that having an objectively superior lifestyle or belief is impossible. As Nietzsche himself said, "There are no facts, only interpretations". This idea was expanded by anti-foundationalist philosophers Heidegger, Wittgenstein and Derrida, who re-examined the fundamentals of knowledge. They argued that rationality was not as clearly defined as modernists and rationalists believed. In addition to philosophers, most psychologists began to exhibit a cognitive bias toward existence, in relation to our default setting of "truth bias". Existentialism is generally considered to be a study in pursuit of meaning in existence and its value to the individual. Unlike other fields of philosophy, existentialism does not treat the individual as a concept, but values individual subjectivity over objectivity. As a result, questions regarding the meaning of life and subjective experience are seen by existentialists as being of the highest importance, above all other philosophical questions.

The main proposition of existentialism is that existence precedes essence; i.e. a being exists before its existence has meaning. Thus allowing us to define ourselves through a process of subjectification. Existentialism undermines epistemology and is the flipside of metaphysics which contends that essence precedes existence. Existentialism is sometimes associated with anxiety, a sense of fear and the awareness of death. It emphasizes behavior, freedom and decision making as fundamental to human existence. This theory is in sharp contrast with both rationalist tradition and positivism. Existentialists argue against descriptions of humans as predominantly rational beings who view reality as solely an object of knowledge. For example, I refuse to view humanity as something that can be regulated by rationalist principles, as we are primarily defined in terms of behavior.

This theory rejects rationalist definitions of being. It also rejects essence as the most common feature that everything in existence has in common. Contemporary existentialists tend to view human beings as subjects in an indifferent, objective and often ambiguous universe in which meaning is not provided by the natural order; but is created by the actions and interpretations of human beings. Although there are common tendencies among existentialists, there are also major differences and disagreements among them. Some existentialists refuse to affiliate with - or even accept the validity of the term. As a result, by the late 20th century, a philosophic movement known as postmodernism emerged. It emphasized a skeptical interpretation of culture, often associated with deconstruction. The term postmodern rapidly gained popularity in literature, music, art, philosophy, economics, and architecture. The term has been applied to several movements in reaction to modernism and is typically marked by a revival of historical elements and techniques. The book you are now reading was originally a postmodern essay, entitled *The Observing Ego*. While writing it, I read a quote about postmodernism made by Albert Arnold Gore.

Dear Albert stated that postmodernism was a perfect combination of nihilism and narcissism (which is ironic, because politicians are usually in denial about both concepts). I immediately took offense to that statement. However, to be honest I wasn't really offended, but that was my only motivation for criticism at that time. I thought to myself, "the nerve of this guy". No wonder so many people think he's a pompous jerk. I doubt that anyone really cares about his opinion on this either way. Al Gore's job titles and pedigree don't impress me. He conceded the 2000 "election" because he was following orders. He was told to step aside, so that's exactly what he did. But in the grand scheme, it doesn't really matter; it was all part of a larger agenda. It wasn't really an "election", it never really is. It's always more of an "appointment". Some people are aware of this dichotomy, yet it doesn't seem to bother them. This could be the nihilism Gore was referring to, but it isn't. Gore believes anarchists such as myself to be nihilistic because he has a misunderstanding of anarchism. In any case, neither he nor any other "pezzonovante" has accurately defined postmodernism as a philosophical movement. Other than a rejection of modernism (which is sometimes ambiguous), it is a rejection of conservative ideology; and the idea that traditional socioeconomics and politics based on reason and objectivity is no longer plausible - because those patterns of social behavior no longer exist. In addition, objectivity and rationale are sometimes diametrically opposed. Objective views are primarily influenced by physical law and mathematic absolutes whereas a rationale can easily proceed from inaccurate information or false assumptions. Either way, those who don't understand how "rational objectivity" is supposed to function (or those who decide to reject it) will presume they exist at the center of the universe. This presumption may be part of the narcissism that Gore referred to, but that doesn't matter. It is not necessary to embrace nothingness if you decide to reject everything, especially because there is no such thing as *nothing*.

A new universe (or multiverse) can be discovered once you forget everything you know about the one in which you currently exist. In other words, <u>nothing is real</u>. We are not bound to this plane of being, corporeally or otherwise. In addition, impossibility cannot exist. Anything that supposedly cannot be done simply has yet to be done. Martial artists will tell you that a flow of kinetic energy (known as Chi) is used to change the density in boards and bricks in order to break them, the same way high pressure storm systems can change the density of a brick wall allowing a block of wood to smash though it. It's not that unusual. These things happen all the time. Just as the time of year in which we are conceived and born affects our patterns of behavior and thought process. So why then do most people stubbornly reject Alchemy, Reiki, Energy Healing, Feng-Shui, Shamanism, Naturopathy and Ancient Astrology – yet easily accept organized religion, theoretical science and "modern" technology? It's because we have been conditioned to believe that natural practices are not sound. We have been led astray from the divine human purpose. As Jordan Maxwell said, "I don't know what God is, but I do know what it isn't". No one can ever tell you exactly who you are or who you are supposed to be. That is for you alone to determine. I am often asked if I believe in God. My answer is yes; but what I believe will always differ from what you believe, even if only slightly. No two systems of belief can be completely identical, but they can share characteristics. This is part of the Gnosis. Human beings are divine creatures with a sacred origin. We all follow a path that we continually create for ourselves; which is also predetermined by something we have absolutely no control over. That seems to be a contradiction, but it isn't. Everything that happens is meant to happen in some way, shape or form. I constantly hear smarty-pants intellectuals complain about how people annoyingly repeat the phrase "everything happens for a reason" yet cannot articulately explain what is meant by that. But guess what? They don't *have* to explain it. The phrase is self-explanatory.

If you disagree, I understand. But no one owes you an explanation for human existence and purpose. You can blame that on whatever you want, or give credit where you think it's due, but life goes on, with or without your participation; active or passive. Contrary to popular opinion, there is no such thing as "the end of the world". The "world" is abstract and therefore has no beginning or end. We merely exist as a part of this abstraction for a minuscule fraction of time; because time is infinite. Time is relative to energy and mass. That's why there is no time in outer space. As a result, mass particles do not merely exist in space-time, they create space-time. In other words, time and space are emergent properties of a gravitational (or electromagnetic) field; existing simultaneously as both the result and cause of all matter in existence. One day, you will cease to inhabit your human form and pass away from this world. On that day, everything you thought you knew will become meaningless. Everything you believed and possessed will become worthless. "The entire world" is something you leave behind, in favor of what comes next. Do I believe in life after death? Yes; but not in this world, not of this consciousness and not related to this element of being. In order to fully understand this way of thinking, you must rise above concepts such as good and evil or even right and wrong. Ethic will always eclipse morality. All around us, on a continual basis, there is negative and positive energy. Neither can exist without the other and we could not exist without both. In our search for answers, we often uncover more questions. The "how" is sometimes easy to understand; the "why" on the other hand, is usually a bit more complicated. The following six monologues each contain several narrative forms. They are not arranged in chronological order. They contain no perception of time. They are descriptive and satirical. They are mythic and autobiographical. They are contextual and metaphoric. To review, discuss and share opinions on the book or to access the online footnotes, please visit skippulley.com

Chapter I

Enlightenment, suffering, fast food; these things seem to be related in some way. Maybe it's a logical progression of unconscious thought - what we *want*, what we *have*, what we can easily *obtain*. But it could also be reversed, as a form of regression; we could easily *obtain* enlightenment if we really wanted it, what we *have* now is suffering, as a matter of course, but what we <u>really</u> *want* is fast food, as instant gratification - to be the gods of our own universe. In both cases suffering is the middle component. Speaking of suffering, here I am…standing in line, yet again. Fast food establishments are Orwellian. As a "reward" for obedience and conformity we are allowed to purchase a food product that is technically edible but not exactly ideal in terms of its content or character. It's my fault for allowing this to happen. Maybe I don't deserve a nutritious meal. But it's not about what we deserve. I will make the best of it, as per usual. I think I will order a "kid's" meal or combo, thereby limiting the damage. I don't mind small portions.

Overall, I'm being pragmatic. I eat fast food when I feel that I'm in danger of starving. This seems to be such an occasion, not having eaten anything at all during the past 24 hours. Although I feel completely lucid, I understand that waiting on line to buy fast food means that I'm probably not thinking clearly. Fast-food restaurant logo colors (typically red & yellow) are designed to provoke anxiety and nervousness, so you won't think about what you're eating. Adversely, fine dining restaurant colors are earth-tones, designed for relaxation and enjoyment. I'm in a local spot right now as opposed to a franchised chain, so I'm feeling the anxiety vibes from the impatient, self-conscious patrons rather than the logo colors. It seems as if everyone is in a hurry except me. Some people are talking loudly on their phone via "Bluetooth" which is ironic. It's a hands-free device…yet they have nothing in their hands. But it's not all their fault. It's an example of conditioned behavior.

Those who don't eat fast food (or an abundance of processed food) are typically smarter, healthier, kinder, more polite and better looking than people who do. Fast food contains high volumes of fat, sodium, sugar and chemical preservatives while lacking vitamins, minerals and fiber. Absorbing the free radicals produced in the preparation of fast food prevents the human body from functioning normally or sending and receiving biorhythms allowing the nervous system to utilize the pineal gland or the "mind's eye"; and that's exactly the point. The calcification and "deactivation" of this gland is very important for maintaining the system of control in our society. As a result of eating artificial, processed food containing chemical additives we have become docile, obedient and suggestible. Our pineal gland is atrophied by age seventeen and made otherwise useless by fast food, television, simulated reality (gaming) and high doses of sugar, caffeine, tobacco and alcohol. Aside from diet and lifestyle, sodium fluoride (which is found in most tap water and all toothpaste), Chlorine, Mercury and Bromide all contribute to the gland's deactivation. Discontinuation or even moderation will begin to reverse the process of toxicity, but reactivation of the gland requires the determination to accept and understand a universal truth of existence. That's the problem. Traditionally, people don't like the truth. Some people actually hate it. The lie is comforting. The lie is a distraction. The lie is the reason so many people are standing in line. I'm part of the lie – although I don't want to admit it. By eating here, I'm also "feeding the archons". But I can't worry about that right now. I need this high-calorie low nutrition kid's combo so I won't pass out. I will contemplate self-awareness some other time. I convince myself it is better than the sugary, non-decomposing, genetically altered meal from the world famous fast-food chain next door. But that is a rationalization. As I step to the counter, a cute young lady lays her "fast food rap" on me; "welcome to blah, blah, blah, our specials today are yak, yak, yak". Shortsightedly, I proceed to order a slightly less harmful children's meal.

"And what to drink", the young Miss asks me in a thick Spanish accent. "Do y'all have fruit punch?" I asked, as she looks as though she has no idea what I'm talking about. It's probably for the best. It would have been loaded with preservatives, high fructose syrup and all kinds of dyes and so forth. It seems like an injustice to even associate it with fruit. "Bottled water is fine", I replied. As I swipe my magic plastic card I realize the young lady taking my order is very attractive. "Are you from South America?" I asked. She smiled and said she was from Peru. "Dynamite!" I think to myself. "That's quality mink" [rubbing my fingers together]. I then suddenly think, "Wow, I hope I didn't say that out loud", although I'm pretty sure I did, as she gives me my order with a slightly embarrassed smile. I say "thank you Ma'am", in my own sincere yet pseudo-patronizing fashion, then I look into the bag to confirm the contents. I wonder to myself about how young she might be. She is the type of girl I would ask out, but the possible repercussions of being rejected by a fast food employee (who may not see me as a viable alternative to taking orders and making sandwiches) is preventing me from being myself right now. Clearly, I'm over-thinking it. I should at least get her number....except....well, I can't. I'm already outside.

What just happened? Was I thinking about all that just now? How long did that take? I stand on the sidewalk for a moment deciding if I should go back. Eventually, I decide against it. The moment has passed. I can always get at her later. She works in the neighborhood, so there will be another occasion to get to know her. I hope. If not, then so be it. It isn't what it isn't. As I walk to my large but mostly empty apartment, I begin to feel that this type of introspective spontaneous thought may have actual merit. We can learn a lot about ourselves through unconscious contemplation of life during the mundane, arbitrary and sometimes pointless tasks we undertake on a daily basis such as waiting in line, reading processed food labels, making small-talk with strangers, pumping gas and sitting in traffic.

This method may not be ideal for a deep understanding of conscious realizations, but if the resulting realization and/or catharsis is genuine, what difference does it make? Maybe that's the point. Maybe Jo Salk had a breakthrough for a polio vaccine when he was outside the lab taking it easy on the sofa or scraping bugs off his windshield or mowing the lawn. It's not a ridiculous notion. I got the idea to start my indie record label by watching two teenage girls fistfight in a parking lot. To this day, I have no idea what the connection could have been. Prior to that I had no intention of forming my own label, but immediately after that I got right to work on it. Maybe I saw it as a symbol of futility from pointless aggression. Maybe there was some degree of sexual arousal involved. I'm not sure. If so, it was on a level high enough to spark a life decision. Ironically, I am opposed to all forms of violence. And although I never wish harm to anyone, I was kind of hoping they would really hurt each other, to teach them both a lesson. But neither were seriously harmed. I'm sure it was eventually forgotten.

It all seemed unpleasant and unnecessary, yet somehow rhythmic and primal. Humans are mammals after all. When animals fight each other, it isn't considered violence because they supposedly lack the ability to reason. If that's true, how is a person who *refuses* to reason any different from an animal? In theory, I guess they aren't. But I could also be rationalizing my lack of empathy or shame in such behavior. In other words, because I don't behave that way - I don't really care what happens to people who do. At least I'm honest about it. When I hear my drunken neighbors outside fighting and arguing, I secretly hope that one of them will pull out a gun and murder the other. That solution works for me; one is dead and the other would probably go to jail. Problem solved, case closed. That's what I call conflict resolution. I realize that would be a negative energy situation, and not exactly in the true spirit of universal oneness (Zen). However, those who listen to reason and think before they react are rarely in those situations.

Believe me, I don't actually *want* anyone to be hurt or killed, but what I want or don't want is irrelevant. Everything happens for a reason. So, maybe other people standing in a line or sitting in traffic right now are thinking about life philosophy, but I doubt it. Almost everyone I know just turns off their brain and watches/listens to commercialized pop-culture horseshit. If and when most people do think about life, do they think about what is real…or what isn't? Other than working, sleeping and putting up with people around them, most people are probably just trying to run out the clock until they die, thinking about things that happened in the past, which could have affected the future. At what point do we stop asking "what if"? That question seems embedded in our psyche. But it really makes no sense. We can't go back and change the past or fast-forward to the future, so we must represent the *now*, on this plane of being. Unless, of course, we *can* change our past, by understanding that time is merely a construct. It doesn't exist.

Al Einstein believed the past, present and future exist simultaneously; in a multidimensional universe. Our physical reality is a *four* dimensional existence. The "now" is no longer objectively represented by space-time. *Now* is the appearance, not the essence. So the question is, would you rather be happy or know the truth? Intelligence and happiness are rarely found in the same place at the same time. This is the key to understanding essence and appearance. No matter how many analytic tools we possess or how philosophically we approach mundane daily tasks, every element of our lives is based almost entirely on appearance. Whether we like it or not, we all make decisions based on judgments - that are in turn based on appearance. I often think about what the existentialists call the "dualism of mankind" which consists of essence (the psychological) and appearance (the physical). I think of essence in its relation to appearance; and if in fact said essence is "pure", if purity even exists. If it does, I can't decide if its purpose is to authenticate, vindicate or justify our existence. It could even be none of the above.

As you can tell, this type of thinking can get deep, quickly. That's probably why most people don't enjoy it. Fortunately, I'm not like most people. I accept that, although it took me a while to understand why. In any case, I'm at home now, and this type of cathartic, free-flow of ideas is suited to my most compulsive ritual - sitting on the carpet, watching old-school antenna television. For some reason, I just don't like comfortable furniture. I can relate to classic "programming" on both a conscious and unconscious level. I absorb the entertainment while my philosophical thoughts meander. So...what is essence? Is it that style vs. substance argument I get into every so often with my friends or is it the anti-appearance - or the "self" buried deep within all matter in the universe? Here are the underlying criterion; essence is considered to be the permanent - as contrasted with the "accidental" element of being, the real or ultimate nature of an object or being diametrically opposed to its existence. Purity is supposedly the quality or state of being pure. It is being thus and no other; sheer and unmitigated. It seems as if purity and essence are very similar and should therefore be afforded the same consideration. But I am convinced that it can't be that simple. In my theory, the "purity of essence" is a manifestation of the dualism of mankind as a reflection of dual truths; the *objective* truth - favoring the physical, and the *subjective* truth favoring the psychological. But like many other theories, I believe there is a flipside alternative. The other side of this construct is the "essence of purity"; a pale, misleading reflection of dual truth that is probably not attainable, but I think that's the point. It's completely opposed to its element of being and rebellious against its ultimate nature. If the state of being pure is "thus and no other", we cannot isolate or even recognize the essence of purity. We would have to believe that most if not all existence is pure. I disagree completely. I believe that no existence is pure. Everything is tainted. Everything is compromised. Everything is imperfect, not accidentally but intentionally, by design; the result of a plan.

The essence of purity – real or not, attracts us to subjective truth. The reason objective truth seems so unattractive is because it is bound by the parameters of the physical realm. In contrast, theoretically speaking, subjective truth can be infinite. It is only bound by the limitations of an abstraction known as the *mind*, in concepts referred to as ideals. Let me give you an example of subjective truth as it relates to the essence of purity and the dualism of mankind. Select any inanimate object at random. Focus on both the object's appearance and its "self" (or essence). That object will ultimately fall into one of two distinct categories: You either accept the object and its essence equally or you reject it. Either you accept that the object is suitable, functional, attainable and accessible – i.e. "it is what it is" or you will see the object as an imperfect version of itself, with its perfect version in existence somewhere in the universe. You can rationalize the process by believing your perception will vary from one object to the next, but ultimately, all objects – from your perspective, will fall into one of those two groups. I am told that this philosophy is counteractive to technological advances.

But in my eyes, without the freedom to create, use and share new technologies freely due to the economic system of control, technology itself is useless and may as well not even exist, i.e. free energy, free life sciences, free healthcare, etc. Before you consider this type of thought to be "absolutist", understand that everything has two sides, or polar opposites. Neither side can exist without the other. And whether you accept it or not, all objects and organisms in the universe are symbiotic. All material matter is in a constant state of movement and/or change. It's curious to me how some people seem to overlook the similarities between the conscious self and the universe, focusing only on the differences, as prescribed by dogma or ideology. I used to think the appeal of ideology was to gain a sense of belonging or possibly reconciliation by reaffirming a set of values. But that could also be an over-analysis, based on my own *lack* of ideology.

My parents once told me that my motivation as a writer made me unique in that I was not driven by any type of ideology, but rather a search for objective truth. I now understand that this search defines my character, but it does not confine my being. Objective truth is a part of the acquisition of wisdom including the capacity to realize what is of value to us. This makes wisdom self-perpetuating; the more you learn - the more you *want* to learn. Wisdom and experience combine to make the best use of available knowledge. Unfortunately in our system, knowledge is often obscured by triviality. A deception created by the system, so that most so-called facts presented to us via the mainstream will automatically support most subjective evidence contextually. This brings us back to subjectivity. Subjective truth is less attractive to me specifically because of this deception. When I draw conclusions from a certain premise to determine what I believe to be true, it is commonly referred to as reason. So why then do I seem so unreasonable? I realize now that I have completely missed an entire episode of *Bonanza* thinking about this. No sweat. I've seen that one before. The *rifleman* is on next.

A lot of people don't realize that the actor who starred in that show, Chuck Connors, played 3 professional sports. He also starred as *Chicken George's* Pop; a Slave Master in the film version of Al Haley's *Roots*. Now dig that, as it relates to essence and appearance; owning your own son. The character of Chicken George in that film, played by Ben Vereen, loses a wager for his freedom betting on a Cockfight. Chuck Conner's character delivers an infamous line prior to that scene; "you're my nigga, George", he said. "You'll always be my nigga". The more I think about that statement, the more profound it seems, especially when set in juxtaposition with the dialectic on today's social norms. I probably hear that phrase 10 times a day. Each time, it has a distinct contextual meaning. Overall the phrase suggests a sense of faith or trust in mutual constraint or the loss/reversal of power and/or control (i.e. I am never "your" nigga, but you are always *mine*).

Dialect is heard and interpreted differently from person to person, the same way that no two people see any one person the exact same way. It is my humble opinion as your narrator that the ability to reason (in addition to setting us apart from the animals) is what binds the essence and appearance to the dual or composite truth (objective and subjective) thereby making the philosophical element of reason the key to understanding how the self relates to truth. The appearance of an object or being may also in fact be the essence, but both essence and appearance are bound by the objective laws of the universe to an observing group and bound by the subjective ideology of any single observing individual. The dualism is our conscious separation from self and the duality is our unconscious unity with self. Both are required for the "self" to function at every level. The self is a construct of pure logic. You don't talk to your self – your "self" talks to you. And it's always correct.

The association of reason and logic are not entirely obligatory because logic is dependent on reason, yet reason isn't necessarily "bound" by logic. Logic is a component of reason, but the two are distinct. It's Ironic that both may become useless in the segregation of essence from appearance. It's like trying to unlock a door with the wrong key; it fits but it doesn't turn. As you have probably guessed by now, dual truths can be frustrating. This frustration can intensify as the dual truth of existence applies to inanimate objects as well as living beings. All matter in existence has a "self", and everything that exists has a flipside. Several years ago, a lady who lived down the street was addicted to yard sales. I mean literally addicted. She would wake her husband up early on Saturday mornings and drag him halfway across town to rummage through the moldy former contents of the garages and attics at the homes of total strangers. Much of said contents had not seen the light of day since being stacked up and locked away in a purgatory of excess until a great rapture brought freedom in the form of lying in rows on the front lawn on a sunny Saturday morning.

I used to stroll to the yard sales within walking distance in search of vinyl records and baseball cards. It was always hit or miss but at least I got some exercise. On one occasion as the lady in question pawed through a box of assorted junk, she came across a ceramic figurine that she simply adored. She asked the homeowner and official yard sale coordinator how much she wanted for it. The rather hefty, genteel woman sporting a straw sun-hat paused for a moment to think it over. She then replied, "Well, seeing as how it's sentimental and all, I'll take five bucks". "Sold!" replied the now infamous vintage and collectible merchandise junkie. Her husband, who would have enjoyed being anywhere else, gave her an extremely hard time, pointing out to her that the $1 and $2 figurines were every bit as good as the one she wanted. She insisted on the five dollar one, sparking a pointless and unnecessary argument fueled by pent-up aggression and lack of communication. Maybe the realization began to sink in for him, of all those lost Saturdays that could have been spent doing anything but pawing through unwanted chachkies and bric-a-brac.

That point is very well taken, but arguing with yard-sale lady (as she became known) was futile. Their argument eventually subsided and she purchased the item with a look of contemptuous satisfaction. She was embarrassed by her husband's behavior, but it would be for the last time. I have always said that if you believe in God you should also believe that he/she/it has a sense of humor. Or poetically speaking, fate has a sense of irony. The lady became curious about the object and after a lot of time-consuming research and extensive conversations with local antiquities dealers; she discovered that the five-dollar ceramic figurine was porcelain and was handmade and hand-painted by a famous 19th century French artist. After a loud public argument over a crummy $5, she was getting what she felt she always deserved, an antique valued in the high five figures. Instinctively, she struck back like the Empire. The Lord, as they say, works in mysterious ways.

She managed to keep this a secret from everyone until after she auctioned off the figurine, stashed the money, filed for divorce and left her husband for another man half his age. When I heard about it, I wasn't surprised. Her husband was a total dick-weed. I heard that he even punched her lights out a few times. I don't know that for sure, but they did argue a lot. A few years later, someone told me he shot himself in the head. But to be fair, in his defense he was also an unemployed alcoholic. After 20 some years of having his house filled with other peoples crap he may have been planning to shoot himself anyway. This merely gave him a reason. It's interesting that money and self-consciousness are often tied to the concepts of reason and rationale in human social behavior. I remember when the word of her amazing yard-sale discovery got around, there was a dramatic increase in people going through their old junk looking for hidden treasure. It seems this nice lady – whom I didn't really know, experienced a completeness of self. In her eyes, from the moment she saw it, the figurines appearance was its essence, thus eliminating the dualism.

Much like objectivity, irony is appealing to me because it always seems to present itself to me without ambiguity. It's immediately apparent to me, but maybe that's just the way I process info. Ambiguity always seems to be my first impression. Life would be less complex if we were all exactly who or what we appear to be, but it would also be extremely boring. Once, while I was walking through a local shopping mall some guy asked me if I spoke English. I looked at him and answered "What country do you think you're in right now?" He turned red and his friends laughed at him, yet he proceeded to ask me for directions which I gave to him cordially. He thanked me and I told him that he was very welcome. I saw that he was embarrassed, so I advised him that next time, unless he is actually in a foreign country - he should probably say "excuse me sir/madam", then ask for directions; *before* questioning someone's ability to articulate the native language. He was indignant at my unsolicited advice.

He was also too embarrassed to say anything else, so he just nodded and walked away. I'm sure he felt that I was trying to be incredibly condescending but the real irony is that I actually wasn't. That's how I really talk, to almost everyone, all the time. Some people (mostly women) who don't know me at all, upon hearing me speak, automatically think I am being defensive in some way or I'm just being a dick, probably based on people they know who speak in a similar fashion. I can understand that. I'm sure they know dicks who sound like me. I am naturally condescending, but I have absolutely no ill intent whatsoever. I do try to smile while when I speak to cushion the jab, but it doesn't always work. On top of that, most people don't understand the basis of my mannerisms and lingo/slang, as my method of speech is particular yet indistinct. I am somewhat unique in this way. Unfortunately, I think ambiguity *is* my ultimate nature (or essence). The purity of which is probably the search for objective truth. I often view pop-culture as a false positive in that many accepted universal "truths" turn out to be completely subjective. History for example, is almost entirely mistaken, fictitious or an outright lie.

Brother Bonaparte said that "history is a set of lies agreed upon". He wrote in his memoirs that "history is written by the winners", which makes perfect sense; dead men cannot tell their own story and defeated men cannot get anyone to listen. H.L. Mencken said "historians are nothing more than unsuccessful novelists" and Oscar Wilde said bluntly that "history is nothing more than gossip". As I stated earlier, there are two sides to everything; a negative and a positive – in every being, in every cell, in every atom - everywhere. In fact, quantum theory is evidence of a two-sided, conscious universe. There are two sides to so-called history, religion, science and mathematics, regardless of their origin. I believe strongly in the concept of negative and positive energy, but I do not believe in the juvenile concept of good and evil; because the only way the concept can be widely accepted is from a child's point of view.

In this sense, understanding the bias of history is very important, as most so-called "evil" deeds perpetuated since the beginning of recorded time were actually in the name of some type of Religion, such as War, Genocides, Ethnic Cleansing, Slavery, Conquest, Invasions, Eugenics and Mass Murder. All because a small group of people convinced a larger group of people to kill and destroy a separate group of people whom they have never even met in the name of serving the will of a higher power or deity. By the very same ideological rationale many religious people believe that atheists are, by definition "evil". This position is understandable from their dogmatic point of view, but given the current religious/monetary system of control it's also completely illogical and generally false. The percentage of people who commit violent crime - who also claim to be an "informed" atheist, is less than 1%.

In fact, the percentage of so-called "intellectual" atheists who are accused or suspected of harming someone for any reason is less than ½ of 1%. Our accepted version of so-called history supports this fact. Since the dawn of recorded history, more human beings have been killed in the name of so-called religion than for any other reason. The Roman Catholic Church considers masturbation a worse sin than rape in some cases. Religious "holy" books have been so misinterpreted that they can justify almost anything anyone does. The Holy Quran can sometimes have up to 50 translations per verse, sometimes varying in meaning. The Babylonian Talmud is loaded with zany rules and nutty conjecture. It's like a cracked magazine combined with a blackface-minstrel joke-book. Based on all that, maybe someone should re-define what "evil" is supposed to be. Oh, wait. I forgot. We can't. Evil is a juvenile concept that can only exist as such - with no questioning of its existence or examination of its cause. In addition to these real life obstacles to enlightenment, there is a tidal wave of digital revisionism adding to the cover-up rather than exposing the truth. The accepted definition of agnostic ("a = without", "gnostic = knowledge") for example, has been revised.

To me it is simply, "outside of the Gnosis" with a possibility of acquiring it, if you so desire. In other words, you may or may not know what God is, but whatever you believe is not exactly what I believe, as our viewpoint of theology is individualized. The newer apologist version of agnostic is that we will never know the truth either way about the existence of God, therefore what you believe is irrelevant (In other words, a skeptic who is too afraid of the possibility of hell to actually call himself an atheist). The irony is, no one's beliefs are relevant. Only behavior has a social impact. In any case, I'm sure there wasn't an agnostic caucus that voted on the change in definition. It sounds more like the language of apologetic atheists who didn't want to miss out on the traditional fun and excitement of jingle bells, Easter eggs, tiny hats, polygamy and systematic genocide. I suppose no one wants to be picked last for dodge-ball. For the record, I'm not an atheist. I'm not an agnostic. I believe in the Great Spirit – which translates as "great mystery". It's not a bearded man who lives on a cloud throwing lightning-bolts, but a collective consciousness of pure energy. I am a spiritual pacifist; completely opposed to firearms, militarism and violence (self-defense is not violence). I believe in natural law and self-symbiosis with nature. I respect the Earth and all things on it, in it and around it. I am a selective carnivore, mostly birds and fish. But I do occasionally eat animals who would eat me if they had the opportunity. My symbiotic attitude toward the animal kingdom is at the basis of my rejection of the good and evil concept, because only *man* can be considered evil – not plants or animals. We are lead to believe that our "superior" intellect as compared to the animal kingdom gives us exclusive rights to a concept that only makes sense to children and people who love being told what to do. To be fair, there are other widely accepted theories and concepts just as illogical as good vs. evil. Evolution, for example describes the processes of natural selection in detail; yet Charlie Darwin skips over the most obvious questions and fills in the gaps with anxiety-fueled speculation.

I think the creationist question "If apes evolved into man, why are there still apes" is reasonable in some sense. Maybe some apes missed the deadline to apply. Maybe they lost their "become a man" voucher because they don't have wallets. Or maybe some apes just decided that it wasn't worth it. Having opposable thumbs seems to be overrated. Humans disassociate themselves from nature more each day. Evolution, like creationism, is just a theory. It is every bit as implausible, without the excitement of an accompanying 1200 page storybook. Granted, Chuck Darwin had a few psychotic disorders, but that doesn't necessarily mean that he wasn't a genius. He may well have been, but even he seemed to realize that some of his ideas were bananas. He once implied that a bear could eventually become a whale in the right circumstances. Then after thinking about it for a while, he changed his mind and said *"No, that's just redankulous. Y'all, don't pay me no mind. I'm crazy for real"*. The problem is, many half-wit intellectuals are so desperate to become the flipside of religious control that they will regurgitate everything Darwin spat out without question. Before you get bent out of shape, I understand that the basic premise is that man and ape share a common ancestor. Although I think adaptation is plausible, there is still no physical evidence of a missing link between man and ape; or that any creature "became" another creature, gradually or otherwise. It's just a theory; as is his theory of how single-celled organisms were created in the first place. A pond, and…bolt of lightning. Really? Charlie was probably a swell fella, but I'm not buying his wolf ticket. There are no absolutes. Some things cannot be explained. Although I do not believe in good and evil, I do believe in dissent and perpetual motion. As a young writer I had been led to believe that Darwinists were inherently "evil", not because they subscribed to the scientific theory of evolution, but because the now discredited philosophy now known as "Social Darwinism" inspired widespread imperialism, to which Marxist Leninist atheism is a response. But this assessment was unfair.

I'm sure various groups of atheists who existed prior to Darwin's work simply adopted his theories to validate their own ideology. From that point of view, who is to say that I (and my contemporaries) am not using existentialism (or postmodernism) the same way - to validate our socio-nihilistic symbiosis of meaning and purpose? It's a fair question. Even I can't answer it. Back when I was "plugged in" to the system, I wanted to write in the transcendentalist style. I thought to myself, "I'm descriptive. I'm down to earth. I love nature. I enjoy wearing a vest. Okay, so maybe I can't grow a cool beard, but I can always buy a hat and a pipe or something". But I had a lot of questions; ones that could not be answered by the color of leaves or the stillness of a pond or the scent of fresh air in springtime. I questioned why I had to be a part of this or any other society, at any level. As I usually posed this question with a calm demeanor, I eventually personified the question in the eyes of many. As a result, I began to judge myself solely on my relationship to my environment, not the people around me.

I basically freed myself - from myself. If we do not or cannot free ourselves, inevitably we will become a perpetual victim of circumstance; the product of subconscious self-reflection. Throughout my adult life, I always tried not to become a self-parody. Eventually, I realized that this was not a legitimate concern. Because parody or not, the truth is what it is. Humans are captives of fear and consumption as a part of system. In my case, I was fully cognizant of my captivity. I was very aware of my "wretchedness of personage" and understood completely that I was a slave. I therefore deliberately "unplugged" myself at an early age. I refused to accept what I was being told by anyone whom I did not trust. I did not accept the authority as truth. I only accepted the truth as authority. It's a lonely existence, but in my eyes it's better than the alternative. When plugged in to the system, we are comparable to lab rats, crawling around an obstacle course. The difference is; if the rats decide to stop running, the course will remain unchanged.

If *we* ever decide to stop running, our system will completely collapse. We perpetuate the system - and the system completely controls us. Johann Wolfgang von Goethe once said "None are more hopelessly enslaved than those who falsely believe they are free." Today we are raised to be excessive materialists from birth. There is no such thing in our society as "enough" – of anything. Wealth, notoriety and fame are not synonymous with happiness yet we are determined to convince ourselves otherwise. Anyone who dares to stand up and tell people that the ultimate goal of life is to find meaning and purpose of self or to practice peace and love is systemically crushed. Although greed, selfishness, and vanity (and by extension capitalism, materialism and competition) are all completely frowned upon by religious dogma, we were taught and still believe that wealth, fame and social status automatically equal fulfillment in life. We are also taught that anyone who disagrees with that notion is mentally ill, or even - dare I say, "Evil". As a result, we intentionally perpetuate the vicious cycles of life. We work ourselves to death so that when we die, we can be buried in a fancy box that costs as much as a used car. We make vain attempts to cheat death and hopelessly combat the effects of aging.

Sociologically we have been brainwashed to work as hard as we possibly can when we're young so that when we get old, we no longer *have* to work and can therefore enjoy "retirement". There is no logic in that. That mentality destroys our youthful optimism. The economic systems of control prohibit us from discovering work that we are meant to do, by forcing us to do work that we feel we *have* to do. Breaking the chains of control would allow everyone to find something they love to do and do it for the rest of their life. Productivity would never be an issue, as all labor would have purpose. Freeing the individual benefits the collective society. If you love what you do, it's not work – it's love. But we rarely get the opportunity or have the motivation to find our labor of love. Instead we settle for pissing our lives away at jobs we can't stand.

The falsely-pragmatic view of this situation is that retirement is better than having to work when you're old. But that's just it, we don't really *have* to work when we're old, because don't *have* to work, ever. As adults, we voluntarily submit to the system in order to remain a part of it. "Working" is a part of that submission in the form of servitude. We work to serve the system - not ourselves or each other. If it wasn't for greed, selfishness and lack of community values, we would all be taken care of in our old age – by our children. The whole point of having offspring is so that we can one day become *their* responsibility. "I helped you up and down stairs when you couldn't walk, now you help me do the exact same thing". It makes perfect sense. Dig it, you're my child; I take care of you, then you take care of me, then I die and leave you money to help fix all the damage you've done to your life thus far. You can buy a car, or get your teeth fixed, or use the extra resources to discover your purpose in life, but more than likely you will just use it to go on a vacation or buy a bunch of crap you don't even need. In any case, when I pass away I'm no longer concerned with the material world you still inhabit.

But understand this; after death, a parents' purpose will shift to the guardianship of your soul, as that is the only part of your being they can influence at that point. A parent's purpose shifts throughout the life of their offspring; from a provider, to a mentor, to a confidant to finally the guiding light of their spirit. Many of you feel that your parents did not live up to those purposes. I understand that. And when they pass away they will understand it as well, more than you can ever know. In death, our spirits have a complete understanding of both life and death. If you forgive yourself for the feelings you are holding on to, and forgive your former providers, mentors and confidants for their mistakes, they will look after your soul for the rest of your life. Allow their spirits to guide you. They are now stronger and wiser than ever, like a Jedi who passes away in the *Star Wars* films, which I believe to be an allegorical myth about the origin of life - and the true meaning of death.

Chapter II

I am typically vilified for writing about the mere suggestion of pure objectivity in society, as if it were not even possible. Former Nazi boiler-stoker Pope Joseph Ratzinger once said, "Pure objectivity is an absurd abstraction". That's funny. I feel the same way about him. Many people today enjoy living in a fool's paradise; dreaming of wealth and fame in the same way stray dogs dream of shelter. Ironically the stray dog has a better chance of reaching its goal; by being adopted - or put to sleep, either way his troubles are over. The rest of us have to continue living in this cave made of denial and virtual reality. But let me hush. It's time for some music. It's beginning to rain. A cool, spontaneous early-spring rain we get in the southeast. The same rain that some feel we never get enough of. Yet, if we ever did, the very same people would then claim that we get too much. So goes the world. I need to hear from my man Arthur Blakey and his Messengers.

I'm considered a purist because I actually listen to vinyl records in addition to collecting them. The truth of the matter is; there is no greater audio fidelity. Although digital reproduction has clarity, it's not about that. It's about the highest highs and the lowest lows. It's about the notes you don't even know you're hearing. It's about the experience. If that makes me a hipster, fine. If I am a beatnik, so be it. I like what I like, and I feel no obligation to compromise. Besides, I have had enough television for a while. At least until *Sanford & Son* comes on. But even that depends on the episode. Television has never controlled me. I control it. I do need to get some writing done, but I probably won't. At least I'm honest about it. Honesty is a trait rarely seen in most people nowadays. Along with integrity and humanity on a socioeconomic level, honesty is almost non-existent. In fact, on the corporate level, honesty is actually counterproductive. A metaphor that corporate-America traditionally uses to describe itself is that of a barrel of apples, with only a few of them being rotten.

In other words, the few "rotten" CEOs who plunder, loot, pillage, murder and steal have no effect on the ripe, sweet delicious ones who plunder, loot, pillage, murder and steal. My metaphor for corporate America is more graphic. I see corporations as a boulder hanging over a politician by a rope held in the hands of Global Banking Cartels. As long as the politician does whatever the bankers want, the boulder stays in place. If not the rope is turned loose and the politician is crushed. The general public, including people calling themselves "voters" never seem to acknowledge any of this. They could if they wanted to, but they always conveniently have their backs turned and their fingers in their ears, whistling Dixie. They do, however see the flattened, blood-soaked corpse of the politician get dragged away by the media as an example of what happens when you disobey the chief executive officer of the cartel. But they always convince themselves and each other that the politician probably just fell down the stairs.

Make no mistake; people who don't know the truth – don't *want* to know the truth, ever. Truth and knowledge of self are counterproductive to what the American dream is supposed to be. No one has ever been placed in a position of power and influence by being themselves. In our neo-fascist, fiat-currency petrodollar economic system, being yourself is the worst possible thing you can be. When set in juxtaposition to the type of person we should be, we are all actually liars, thieves and con-artists. We are prisoners of consumption, fear and insecurity shuffling across the stage of life's auditorium. We yearn for applause from the masses, but in the end we only hear ridicule and icy silence. The social systems that control us, the ones that we perpetuate, have devoured the kinder elements of our being. That's how we get sayings like "doing the right thing for the wrong reason" and vice versa. Social development and intellectual growth both draw from negative and positive elements of our society. We utilize aggression, assertion and agitation as much as patience, understanding and empathy - in problem solving and basic human interaction.

But there is always a variable; that ever-present element, the wild animal known as human emotion. Sometimes it's a blindfold, sometimes it's a microscope. Sometimes it is background noise. But it is often an impediment to truth. You may not like my theory of composite truth, but the bottom line is that objective truths are concerned with a person's being; while subjective truths are concerned with a person's *way* of being. I am complicit in this duality. I refuse to adopt universally accepted truths; understood by most yet expressed differently from one person to next. The by-product of which is the basis of symbolism, which conveys meaning but also represents character; which is most evident when symbolism is either mistranslated or misunderstood. If I walk around with a swastika on my briefcase, I may be a WWII historian, I may be a German antiquities collector, but I'm probably just an asshole. Even though I understand perfectly well that it is actually an ancient sun symbol of well-being, most people would wonder why a Native American-Negro would advocate the National socialists. The Wall St. Cronies who financed the Nazi party suggested they co-opt the symbol specifically to subvert the traditional meaning of it. We must learn to trust our instincts and use our common sense. Socially, we learn to despise hypocrisy yet we continually practice it as a matter of course. We are institutionally raised to bully and swindle in order to gain advantage yet we revile those concepts when presented as ethic. Humans, unlike most other animals are inevitably drawn toward the unknown, whereas animals only have a natural curiosity about their physical surroundings. Animals don't care about what's true, they only care about what's real – at least from their point of view. We are told this distinction stems from our ability to reason, but how much truth (if any) resides in that ability? How much reality resides in truth? Perhaps humans should incorporate more of the simplicity found in nature. I'm not sure if that would strengthen my opinion of dual truth or force me to abandon it. That's probably how the phrase "too simple to be true" originated.

An old saying about truth ascribed to one of the biblical John's, (there were at least 4 Johns in the bible) "the truth will set you free", is a strong implication that without an understanding of truth - or the willingness to seek it, we are either a prisoners or slaves. I also like the saying "freedom or death" because it implies that those two things are in some way synonymous. A complicated element of truth is that some of the things we believe to be true usually depend on our mental capacity to hold a distinct piece of information; the gathering of which may sometimes consist of memory alone. Memory, as we all know is often flawed and typically influenced by several factors. Most young people today find it very difficult to separate their actual memories from stories they read online or images they see in movies or on television shows. Large media corporations bombard the masses with a mainstream pop-culture "Psy-Op" or psychological operation, making it difficult to separate reality from make-believe.

With the advent of augmented reality, that line may be completely obscured once and for all. Mass Media is basically telling you that truth does not exist, and even if it did exist, it doesn't matter. In mainstream media, a rectangular screen is your God. You *must* – under all circumstances, do what the screen tells you to do; Buy, Wear, Drive, Eat, Drink, Play, Work, Believe, Support, Love, Hate, and Worship what the screen tells you to. Why? Well, it's simple. The screen tells you exactly what's wrong with you constantly; and there always has to be something wrong with you. According to the screen you are never okay. You're fat, you're ugly, you're poor, you're dumb, you're sick, you're unpopular, you smell bad and no one likes you; because that's what the screen displays on a continual basis. Above all, don't ever question anything the screen says and never trust anyone who does. This is a classic formula. In the years leading up to WWII, several prominent Wall St. bankers who were instrumental in creating the 3rd Reich, wrote guidelines for German propaganda to protect their financial interests.

For example, the quotation; *"If you tell a lie big enough and keep repeating it, people will eventually come to believe it. The lie can be maintained only for such time as the State can shield the people from the political, economic and military consequences of the lie. It thus becomes vitally important for the State to use all of its powers to repress dissent, for the truth is the mortal enemy of the lie, and thus by extension, the truth is the greatest enemy of the State."* The accuracy of this statement is evidence of revision. This quote is usually attributed to Joseph Goebbels, (who coincidentally was raised as a Jesuit) however it is unlikely that he wrote this, because Goebbels actually *believed* the bullshit he was spouting. If, as a "true believer" he ever acknowledged that his rhetoric was a lie, it would defeat the entire purpose of his propaganda. In other words, he wasn't that clever. By definition, no one can prove a lie; therefore certain proofs must be manufactured to fit a particular ideology or dogma. God, for example, is considered to be a supreme reality by those who believe in it. However, for those who do not, it is sometimes easy to override emotions attributed to divine inspiration by using their objective knowledge of known psychological conditions and natural bio-chemical reactions. Some people overcome their fear or curiosity of an omnipotent being simply by denying its existence and embracing a purely scientific view of the universe. We are afraid of the dark because of the unknown and we avoid the absence of light in general out of instinct. Is one reaction completely emotional and the other completely rational? They are both a means to the same end. In this sense, truth is only important to the individual. The god Prometheus may have been nothing more than a lightning storm but that has no bearing on the outcome. For Eons we have slept in the dark and thrived in the light of day. So perhaps fear of the dark is a rational fear. Our contempt for the future is exemplified by the same rationale. Very few ancient cultures had a word that meant "daily" but they all had a word that meant "tomorrow", because they knew very well that every day may be their last.

Why does it seem nihilistic to acknowledge that there may not be a tomorrow? We always expect it, but we can't guarantee it. Life is only half of the equation, death is the other. After death, the "gnosis" is complete, A+B=C, or life + death = gnosis. Science and God become irrelevant. All accepted science may be proven false. God may be exactly what each individual believes it to be – or not to be. We all may be eternal beings, with no beginning or end. Our existence may be our own (or someone else's) imagination. Life may indeed be just a dream. Gnostic dualism may be nothing more than the existence of good requiring the existence of evil to define itself. Just as the mind requires the brain, or the spirit requires the body. "God" may just be a metaphor for pure consciousness. The "truth" may just be physical information processed by the brain then abstracted by the mind. From this duality of consciousness we derive the ability to rationalize our behavior while believing in a higher power. Our understanding and acceptance of our human insignificance propels us forward and holds us back simultaneously. The theory that God's existence is unknowable is in direct opposition to the existentialist question "who am I" in favor of the postmodernist question "what am I". If that is the case, are we obligated to justify our existence, as the end must justify the means? No, because our existence is a means to an end. Most species of animal on Earth believe that when they see a reflection of themselves it is actually another animal. At times our own reflection seems opposed to our existence, so we convince ourselves that it is just another animal. We acknowledge the dualism instead of the duality. No matter how we see ourselves, others will still see us differently, even if only slightly. It is much easier to avoid "the other animal" than it is to examine our appearance as it relates to our essence. Again, in this instance, truth only matters to the individual. It may or may not be true that you're fat – but it's *real* that you just split your pants. My favorite saying in regards to truth is "the truth is found between the lies" because that makes perfect sense to me.

In my experience, a lie is often worse than the circumstances which precipitate it. In other words, lies are among the most incriminating evidence. Paul Gerhardt said "When a man lies he murders some part of the world". He understood the meaning of truth. The effect of the lie on your character may not be immediate, but the buildup of lies always substantial. The lie of a generally honest person not only damages their credibility (for what it's worth) but also affects the way they look at themselves and others. That's probably why habitual liars are so at ease in social situations, because they cannot look at themselves objectively in any circumstance anyway. By that logic, it is more difficult for those who seldom lie to psychologically recover from it. If your principles are continually compromised, the next thing to fail is your integrity. After that, only your manhood or womanhood remains. Therein lay the basis for adopting a set of values – *any* set of values, regardless of how moral you believe them to be.

Always remember that so-called morality is subjective. No two people will view the same set of morals in exactly the same light. That is the real value of understanding spiritual individuality. Just because most of the people you know and love have a particular set of values does not mean that you have to automatically adopt them, especially after becoming an adult. My individuality is the central component of my character; it's a separate objective existence. If I allow my character to be compromised by a system of values that greatly favors the group rather than the individual on a spiritual level, I will lose my ability to express myself without a majority of bias - on any level. Objectivity is vital to building individual character. I am very careful not to let my emotions influence my way of thinking. But I am human after all. Emotion has a purpose in life. We have them for a reason. The same way we have teeth to chew and limbs to ambulate. The difference is, sometimes we control our emotions and sometimes our emotions control us. This affects our intuition and how often we choose to follow it.

As a child, my parents taught me that there is an "ethical" force at work inside all of us and throughout the universe. Those who choose to intentionally oppose this force will eventually be destroyed; literally or figuratively. Human history as we know it, if you read between the lines, seems to demonstrate this point. Ethics, from the Greek word "*ethikos*" simply means "arising from habit". It is also branch of philosophy which includes analysis of concepts such as right and wrong, good and evil, and responsibility. The simplicity of these concepts is the very core of their essence. Most people accept them for the same exact reason I reject them. In my opinion, God is simply how we define our humanity. But this is a balancing act. If you believe that God is the supreme reality and the sustainer of the universe, you should also accept God as your source of moral obligation. By not doing so, God becomes a weapon instead of a tool. Instead of a really awesome invisible friend who is always supporting and protecting you, God becomes a clinical narcissist who requires constant reciprocal praise and attention. Sig Freud regarded the universal sustainer view of God as "wish fulfillment" for the perfect father figure, while Marxist writers see it as powerlessness experienced by men and women in oppressive societies. The truth is somewhere in-between. What I refer to as the living universe, or Great Spirit is referred to by most as *God*, but I neither worship nor praise it in the traditional sense - because my "God" does not ask for, expect or require it – and probably wouldn't appreciate it. I am sometimes referred to as a "Pantheist" because pop culture loves social labels; especially to describe things that most refuse to accept or understand. But dig this well, I'm not trying to convince anyone of anything. You must come to your own understanding. If you do not want your "self" to be symbiotic with nature, that's your decision. Your beliefs do not affect my behavior. Your behavior does not affect my spirit. It is infinite and one with the universe. You can run with - or get run over by the universe; in either case it will continue, with or without your participation.

Social labeling stigmas contribute to people's lack of understanding about the living universe theory. In the context of philosophy I am often asked whether I subscribe to evolution or creationism – as if those are the only two choices for the origin of mankind. To be honest, I don't really subscribe to either one. The "Darwin worship" of accepted evolution omits the necessary details of how life was originally began and although very close, the parables and coded analogies of human creation woven into the allegorical myth of the biblical storybook still mismatch my own theory. No human can or will ever fully understand the truth of human origin. Our time biologically in this world - on this plane of being is just one half of the human "coin". The flipside is death, in which the rest of human existence is instantly revealed. I believe that human beings have a "divine" origin, which is evidenced most clearly by our lack of symbiosis. However, to be fair, most ancient cultures were more symbiont prior to widespread systemic control. Some "modern" cultures are seen as having slightly more of a mutually beneficial relationship with nature, but in the long run, that is inconsequential. In a "civilized" society, everyone takes more from nature than they give back because they have no other choice. It's systemic. Some have the arrogance to believe that our unsustainable, runaway system of production and consumption can be somehow reversed or mitigated via "save the earth" campaigns. But "Climate shift" is occurring because it is simply due to occur. The extraction and dependence on petroleum has stained and corrupted human existence, but I can assure you, the "earth" can and will save itself, just as it has on at least 5 prior occasions. Climate change is not the end of the world, just the end of *us*, and rightfully so. The earth is tantamount to a living being, in a living universe. It will simply eradicate us then reset itself, for the 6th time. "Tohu wa bohu" or "waste and desolation" is key to understanding the gnosis. It is evidence that the gnosis can never be possessed or kept secret, only shared. Open-source spirituality stems from reason, while proprietary religion stems from rationale.

When I think about reason versus rationale, I think of how I get kind of fat every couple years. Although not quite as fat as my heroes Orson Wells, Patrice O'Neal or Big "Ern" Hemingway, just fatter than I probably should be. The irony is that I am not a big eater. My diet is usually very good. I just have a very low metabolic rate. As I get older, the rate gets even lower. Under normal circumstances I am very active. Without a high level of activity, my body stores an excessive amount of fat. I suppose this is true of most people. But I seem to exhibit a constant state of gaining or losing. This has become known as "weight cycling". I am never really that concerned with actual weight, just with looking fat and not fitting into my clothes. The last time I traveled extensively for work, I had to wear gym clothes and track suits because I couldn't fit into my fashionable business attire. Prior to my last trip, while trying to put on a pair of slacks, I strained to fastened them, then the fly-button flew off with so much force it cracked a small mirror.

As I stared at the cracked mirror in concerned fascination, I thought of how most people simultaneously overanalyze and oversimplify situations and events. We have discovered that it is much easier to rationalize any given situation than to find any real reasons for it. My rationalizations for getting fat were as follows: I didn't have time to work out (that's a lie), I didn't have the opportunity to cook (that's true, but restaurants also offer low-calorie meals) or I was under a lot of stress (that one is my favorite). Ultimately, those are just excuses. I gained weight because I ignored my normal diet and lifestyle. I'm not running from that reality. I'm human, after all. I admittedly enjoy the occasional refreshing adult beverage. I'm not continually concerned with my health, although I'm probably more concerned about it than Ernie Hemingway was. These things happen. I don't sweat it. I just pick myself up and get going in a new and better direction. More activity, smaller, healthier food portions and fewer P's & Q's at the pub and I buttoned those slacks with absolutely no problem.

I did have to go buy a button at a fabric store, but I sewed it on myself because I am resourceful. I am a former scout. Our symbol was the *"fleur di lis"*; which was later completely co-opted by the Bourbon Kings of France (speaking of fat, lazy drunks) who claimed it as their family coat of arms. I remember as a child that pissed me off a little. Everyone knows the Sons of God/Heavenly Council-Brothers gave that symbol to my main man Clovis! Well, I can't be sure that actually happened. I just read it somewhere. It's not a strong conviction. But if it was; it would be an example of how rationalization can be potentially dangerous, especially when based on hate and fear. If the practice of constantly making excuses goes unchecked or becomes institutionalized, then a false rationality becomes a motivating factor. So, corporations routinely tell puppet politicians to tell "the public" to send poor people halfway around the world to kill even poorer people and gloriously die to protect the "American way of life".

Before you get your knickers in a knot, I realize that many other Countries also have long lists of committed atrocities, but those countries also seem to *learn* from their mistakes. Americans love to rationalize. Who's to say that rationale won't come back to bite you in the ass? Oh, that's right. It already has – and it will continue, unless the culture of fear and consumption is destroyed. That is unlikely however, because that culture also fuels the engine of society. Like most Americans, I was bombarded with fear and hate based rationale while I was growing up. Keep in mind; a "fear induced rationalization" is not the same as a "rational fear". When I was very young, I read something interesting about Brother Napoleon I Bonaparte. In case you have been misinformed as to his true identity, let me hip you to it. It is unique to say the least. During his career he was the Emperor of the French, the King of Italy, the Mediator of the Swiss Confederation and the Confederation of the Rhine. He was a general of the French Revolutionary Army and the ruler of France as First Consul of the French Republic.

Over the course of little more than a decade, the armies of France under his command fought almost every European power (often simultaneously) and acquired control of most of continental Europe by conquest or alliance until his disastrous invasion of Russia in 1812. His innovations revolutionized warfare; from the divisional squares employed in Egypt to the placement of artillery into batteries. His campaigns are studied at military academies all over the world and he is widely regarded as one of the greatest commanders who ever lived. But aside from his military achievements, Napoleon is also remembered for the establishment of the Napoleonic Code. Also known as the French Civil Code, it was the first successful codification of Civil Law. He pioneered Modern Egyptology, founded the Bank of France and the Paris Stock Exchange. He unified and reorganized Germany, gave Poland National Identity, adopted the metric system, emancipated the Jews, commissioned Robert Fulton to invent the submarine and doubled the size of a Crown Subsidiary Corporation called the United States. Yet, despite all of those achievements, as schoolchildren we were taught that Napoleon was a tiny madman and tyrant who wanted to take over the world because he was only five feet two inches tall. (In actuality, he was 5'6" tall, which was a normal height for a man of his time.) We were being taught to rationalize how or why someone could achieve goals which for his time seemed impossible rather than engage in logical reasoning about how or why they were achieved. Society has created such a rationale about who they think he was that an actual psychological complex has been associated with him. If having this condition means spreading enlightenment, equality and revolutionary ideas to half of the world, then I would not mind having a Napoleonic Complex. But like Bonaparte, I never define my accomplishments based on society's definition of success. I simply create my own. Napoleon was able to define his accomplishments because he was a brilliant military strategist.

War is the oldest organizing principle in society. War is the basis of how so-called history is recorded and remembered. When the European monarchies united to crush the revolution in France, Bonaparte handed out whippings and speed-knots to every country in Europe for nearly 20 years. That *will* tend to cause a lot of sore feelings. So it is unlikely that historians in the countries he conquered are going to remember him as a swell fella. It's also pretty hard for average citizens to pay attention to the advancement of social enlightenment when your country is wearing its ass for a hat. I'm sure Napoleon did things he shouldn't have done, but that doesn't change what he accomplished. He also understood duality. In some cases, Napoleons reason for war also happened to be his rationale. Lazare Carnot, the French engineer, mathematician, Freemason and Minister of War once wrote "War is a violent condition; one should make it to the utmost or go home". When I read that, I thought that the statement was too simple to express the overall impact of war on an individual or collective society.

But I now understand that it is a reasonable statement about the condition of war, not a rationalization of why wars should or should not be fought. We need to look past the appearance (rationale) straight to the essence (reason). In fact, in this case, you can ignore the rationale completely. For Napoleon these two were actually one in the same, thus eliminating the dualism. For Carnot, they were distinctly opposite or paradoxical. I understand that now. I was previously reading this quote as an anti-war sentiment instead of its original intent, which describes the act of "total war". I was mistakenly looking at the pretext of starting war as a violent condition and the consequences thereof – instead of the behavior one should exhibit when confronted with warfare in the physical sense. From its inception in the mid-19th century, the concept of total war was accepted as the most logical way to achieve military (as well as economic) victory when two or more countries are engaged in war with each other.

"Total war" is the practice of intentionally making war on the civilian population and civil industry; the backbone and support of armed forces and fighting troops. The only logical conclusion to this theory of warfare is to either destroy everything in your path or not make war at all (i.e. make war to the utmost or go home). A rationale is typically an argument for or against. Reason provides the actual purpose. A rationale is sometimes a "reasoned" argument to justify a course of action. However in modern times it is typically just an excuse given to the masses by political leaders to explain why a particular action was taken, especially when the action turns out to be a mistake. Reason is a term used in the philosophy of arguments to refer to the ability of the human mind to form and act on concepts in conformity with rationality and logic. Logic is not the same as reason. They are distinct, although logic is an important aspect of reason. The modern tendency to prefer what is called "hard logic" has incorrectly led to the terms being viewed as synonymous. Even more often, logic is seen as the defining or pure form of reason.

I believe that most people in our society will attempt to rationalize a lie by stoutly defending irrational and illogical theories while proceeding from false assumptions. More importantly, people in positions of so-called authority will simply categorize the lie as a mistake or accident. Our system creates such inertia toward rationalizing an unreasonable (and often ridiculous) concept that most people completely overlook reason in favor of the rationale. I always seem to use war as a point of reference because it contains so many false paradigms. War something that almost everyone will agree is a bad thing, but almost no one agrees is either unavoidable or unnecessary. However this is a false presumption; war is both avoidable and completely unnecessary, but there is a reasonable explanation for why most people arrive at the opposite conclusion. We must first look more closely at the geo-political and economic systems that have been adopted by most countries in the world.

These systems perpetuate a rationalization that will always proceed from a false set of circumstances. We are taught from day one by the control systems that war has multiple causes. As a series of related sociological events are concerned, this sounds true, but it isn't. The condition of warfare has but one cause and is perpetuated for one reason and one reason alone; Socioeconomic materialism and possession. The control and domination of a world populated by consumers, i.e. wage/debt slaves or systemic prisoners, by a handful of world banking autocrats who decide when, where, how and why all wars will be fought. This is true of all wars, from the very first war to the wars currently in progress. Every major conflict in the history of mankind has been linked to some form of possession. In fact, the original act of violence as portrayed in the bible (Cane vs. Abel) was over the "possession" of God's favor. To understand the significance, we need to examine possession in both forms; concrete and abstract. A material possession is any item or property owned by a "person" or group of people. The key is, you *must* first attain personage to "own". It is therefore crucial to the system that you become a person (or corporation) and reject humanity. A Political possession is a territory under the control and sometimes protection of a larger Country, which is not considered a part of that country. Guam for example, became a political possession of the US after beating up Spain and later Japan for control of it. And last but by no means least; Spiritual possession refers to the ability of spirits - such as those of good or evil to inhabit a human body. I will start with the last one first. This is a misunderstanding of possession in general and of spirits in particular, which are neither good nor evil. Spirits do not *possess* the body; they commune with the "self". Anyone who claims to be possessed is usually either brainwashed or mentally ill. Although fundamentalists often claim to channel the Holy Spirit - and Spiritualists often allow spirits to guide them via meditation, when someone is said to be "possessed", the spirits in such cases are generally regarded as "evil".

This is unique because most other forms of abstract possession do not share the same negative connotation; such as possessing a sense of confidence, community, pride, self-worth or accomplishment. One could argue that possessing a sense of superiority or being self-possessed could be negative, but it could also be a benign personality trait or an equalizing component in building one's character. It is an interesting debate, but I would much rather confront someone who is self-possessed rather than someone who desires more and more material possessions; as the desire for material possessions is perpetual. The more you acquire – the more you *require*. The more you get, the more you want because we are taught that there is no such thing as enough. A strong sense of material ownership is for those who are spiritually insecure. It is part of an institution of coercion compelling humans to withdraw from community. You may think that is absurd, but based on the effects of violence on human psyche, it is completely logical.

When we examine the given causes of war, we find only hypothetical rationale, usually based on events we cannot even confirm. This rationale is then built up and sold to the average citizen who as a result, does <u>all</u> of the fighting, killing and dying. Unfortunately most people still view war as a series of military campaigns between two opposing armies over some type of sovereignty, territory, resource, religion, or ideology. Selling this false pretense of war to the working class is necessary in order for them to digest the rationale of why wars are fought, and why the poor have to fight them. The bottom line is; war is always a rich man's war but a poor man's fight. The ever-present weapon of emotional manipulation must be utilized to convince everyday people that violence and bloodshed is a viable component to sustaining or improving their present condition. Keep in mind, no matter how many flags are waved, politicians, corporatists and people of above average income do not enlist in the military or send their offspring to fight, they send *you and yours*; the poor, the uneducated, the misguided and misinformed.

46

The economic motivation for the rich to make war is filtered and siphoned into an economic and civic rationale to convince working class people to take on the actual fight. These rationalizations sometimes lead to a paradox. Wars of "independence" sometimes overlap with wars of "liberation". War between internal factions within a state or country is ironically called a "civil war", which is like a rhetorical oxymoron. Unless someone hands out cool uniforms or everyone mutually agrees on scarf/hat combos before the fighting begins, it's difficult to know which side everyone else is on. Southern boys ran into that problem at Bull Run in 1861. Research suggests that at some point during the battle, everyone was shooting at almost anyone. I can't blame them, really. One can never be too careful in Manassas. Prior to World War II, Nations would usually issue formal declarations of war, but in modern times the nature of war has changed dramatically. Today there are other more convenient terms for war, often used euphemistically to circumvent the psychological impact of or legal limitations on warfare. These include "armed conflict", "hostilities", and "police action". In the modern age, the equivocation of war necessitates the complexity of peace.

As Baruch Spinoza once said, "Peace is not an absence of war; it is a virtue, a state of mind, a disposition for benevolence, confidence, and justice." Instead of selling the public on irrational and sometimes ridiculous causes for national or regional wars, wealthy industrialists and bankers now try to sell people on "Global" wars, which is always reasonable from their point of view despite any given rationale. George Orwell once wrote, "Wars are not meant to won, they are meant to be continual." The real war is being waged against society by the ruling-class elite. War - or at least the preparation and willingness to engage in war, is seen as a "necessity for defense" of one's country. Ancient philosopher Vegetius wrote "He, who wishes for peace, let him prepare for war". But if that were true (or reasonable), why do nations who arm themselves to the teeth seem to provoke conflict very soon after doing so?

To answer that, let's try to define war in common terms. Traditionally, a war is two or more armies fighting one another in the "field". The invasion of a sovereign nation - provoked or not, was usually the pretext. So the paradigm of being armed to prevent war doesn't really apply, unless you just happen to be expecting a group of assholes to attack you for no apparent reason. But therein lay the rub, because there is *always* a reason - and it's always the same exact reason; possession and imperialism in the form of conquest. At some point, ancient civilizations began to war against each other as feudal materialism eventually gave birth to imperial conquest. The biggest difference between those cultures and ours, besides the inhumanity of technological warfare, is the fact most of the enlightened minds of ancient cultures were aware of their nations systematic subjugation of other lands, whereas most contemporary intellectuals of are willfully ignorant of Anglosphere empire building or simply decide to rationalize it.

The United States of America, technically a Corporation, has become the staging point for world domination. This has nothing to do with people or ideology and everything to do with resource based economics and the system of control. You can get into infinite arguments about what the US is, was or should be, but nothing can change the fact that the native inhabitants of the Americas were systematically annihilated to possess the land on which this corporation is built. The so-called US war of independence was actually just another British civil war, between an army officially representing the crown corporation against another representing its subsidiaries. Because both sides were secretly funded by the same sources, the resulting "Nation" was an even more powerful representation of the Crown's worldwide interests. In a post-revolutionary North America, a group of "Globalists" now had the motive, means and opportunity to truly conquer the rest of the world. The destruction of natives continued under westward expansion, while the importation of African and pacific Island slaves kept the engine of conquest on track.

As an interesting footnote, the word "British" is thought by some revisionists to be derived from the Hebrew words "brit" meaning *covenant* and "ish" meaning *man*, which in Hebrew reads as "man of the covenant". That could just be a linguistic anomaly, but I doubt it. In any case, there's no better rationale for a group of people to attempt domination of the entire world than because they believe God *wants* them to do it. It's like a built-in excuse for abhorrent behavior. For this reason, many progressive intellectuals have a seething contempt for the geopolitical movement now known as "Zionism"; whose nationalist roots can be traced back to Central Europe, but whose economic foundation was codified in the UK, financially backed by powerful banking families based in inner London. In my opinion, the intended purpose of the Zionist movement was to create an alternate or secondary base of operations, located in the middle east. This would explain why Israel received billions in aid from the UK and US. It's basically "payroll" from management to its employees. This is also why the enemies of Israel are also coincidentally enemies of the Anglosphere.

Funny how that works. But in the long run, imperialism is still just a symptom of the underlying disease; the monetary and religious systems of control. If by chance a secret cabal of globalists succeeds in destroying humanity for any reason, they will have done so because you opted to support rather than resist them. When Brother Bonaparte met with Tsar Alexander at Tilsit on a raft in the middle of the Nemur River in 1807, The first thing he said to him was "all Russian trade with the British must stop". It was long rumored that in reply, Alexander whispered to him in French "I hate the English as much as you". But what he really said, in Russian, according to Napoleons translator, was "every Englishman is a Jew". Why would Alexander make such a sweeping (and seemingly off-topic) indictment if he didn't think it was relevant? I don't think it was meant as hyperbole. Al wasn't that clever. The *Treaty of Tilset* which they both signed that day was an agreement to enforce a continental trade embargo of Britain.

In spite of this, Alexander still allowed prominent Russian industrialists to secretly trade with the British in violation of the treaty, until he finally broke the treaty outright in 1810. He claimed that the blockade was ruining the Russian economy, but in my opinion, he needed US and British-made materials and cash from sales of hemp as leverage against the Rothschild's, who were trying to form a central bank in Russia. Alexander and Napoleon were the only two European monarchs who were not deeply in debt to the Rothschild's; with the possible exception of King George III of Britain, whose health was rapidly deteriorating (and may also have been a victim of continual arsenic poisoning). I think both Alexander and Napoleon partially misunderstood the other's relationship with the Rothschild banking clan; each believing the other could not control them. As it turns out, they were both correct.

In 1812 the Rothschild's maneuvered their way into control of the Bank of France, while simultaneously funding the British Crown Corporation's reinvasion of North America to re-establish their interests after the US Central Bank charter expired the year before. The Rothschild's now directed all their resources into destroying Napoleon, who had become their greatest threat. They financed the British army during the Spanish Peninsula campaign and as Bonaparte retreated from Russia and the French army began to disintegrate, all of Europe came in for the kill. In 1815 The Rothschild's took control of the UK stock market following the battle of Waterloo by deceiving traders into believing that Napoleon had actually won the battle. Although Russia had avoided the setup of a Central Bank for the time being, the Rothschild's secretly plotted yet another banking takeover in the US, and swore revenge on the Tsar and all his descendants. A century later they would exact this revenge by supporting the Bolsheviks in the Russian Revolution and manipulating Woodrow Wilson into allowing the creation of the Federal Reserve. The 1812 re-assimilation of the US colonies back into the Anglosphere had cemented the US as the archetype for corporate control and manipulation.

Imperialism flourished, disguised as defending "freedom". The US attacked Mexico to take California. The "union" invaded the Confederate states to perpetuate the myth (and create a new myth) of freedom. The US attacked Spain to take Cuba, Puerto Rico, the Philippines and Guam. The US/UK provoked both "World Wars" to protect international banking interests of the Banking Cartels and prevent first the Ottoman Turks and later Germany from becoming new archetypes for industrial world power. The US invaded Vietnam, Panama, Iraq (twice) and Afghanistan as directed by the "military industrial complex" which is a subsidiary of the World Bank and IMF; directed by the Ruling Class of the Corporatocracy. Do you see a pattern developing? Try to understand that all so-called "provocation" is merely a pretext - and is usually a contrived incident or presented to the public with a total lack of evidence; The Rio Grande, Fort Sumter, the USS Maine, the Lusitania, the Gulf of Tonkin, global "terrorism", ethnic cleansing, thus and so. These rationalizations presented as a cause lead some people to believe that certain wars which they view as "just" are not only legitimate but also the responsibility of organizations such as the United Nations to regulate and control. This is a complete misunderstanding of the true cause of war, which is always economic. World organizations have no more legal or moral standing to judge the validity or support the rationale of a conflict than any single sovereign nation. Even if they did, it wouldn't matter because any supposed "cause" given to the public or a world organization will be exaggerated or false. It's not in the best interest of those who profit from war to tell you the truth about it. You will never see a bumper-sticker that says "let's send poor and lower middle-class teenagers to die in the desert so the rich can get richer". Just as you never see fast food ads saying "eating here will lead to obesity, heart disease, arthritis and diabetes". You can't sell fast food with honesty and integrity and you can't further the goal of world imperialism by informing everyone that it is in fact happening.

This brings us back to the concept of "total war"; the modern term for the intentional targeting of civilians as well as the mobilization of an entire society. Because each member of society must contribute to the war effort, they are therefore strategically targeted. This harsh reality crushes the paradigm of romanticism in war. However, this is a completely reasonable way of viewing warfare that could easily be rationalized as a necessity, especially by those who are doing the actual fighting. It was originally employed during the US Civil War, then re-tested successfully in the Franco-Prussian War and eventually perfected in WWI. However, the concept of total war is not quite as good for business as traditional war by those who create and profit from it. It's already difficult to re-assimilate after fighting in a war you just lost, but it's impossible if you and everyone in your community are dead. Because those who create war can never conceive of eliminating it, they did the next best thing; they changed the "nature" of war by creating the psychological effect of a constant threat, i.e. "terrorism".

The creation of an imminent and continual threat eliminates the necessity to sell a cause for war to the public. In addition, we are at a point in which multinational corporations no longer need a majority of the public to actively support their wars. As long as a significant number of people are willing to continue their daily routine and specifically not oppose war, then the war machine will continue unabated. Keep in mind, my point of view is that of someone who is completely nonviolent with no allegiance to any flag or corporation. I do not believe in the idiotic concept of drawing lines on the earth (of which we all belong) and exclaiming "this part is mine - and that part is yours, and we will always recognize differences and similarities based on these arbitrary lines". I especially do not believe in invading lands where civilizations already exist and thrive as a culture in order to murder them all and take it for yourself (despite the fact that they initially welcomed you and just gave you part of it). That's pure psychopathy. That's the US.

Guardians of the control systems drew lines on the earth as "borders" ambiguously based on culture and language. I am not bound by any natural law to recognize them. It is not my intent to debate nationalism, patriotism or the effect of empire on society. My intent is to expose war and violence as a paradox illusion. It is the physical, tangible expression of a deeper human conflict. There is a prevalent psychological theory that war and violence are innate to so-called human nature. The big problem with that is human *nature* does not exist, only human *behavior*. We are merely reacting to our environment. In my opinion, as a result of our modern economic control system, it is pointless to analyze patterns of violent or antisocial behavior or try to change or modify what war has become. We are only lashing out at the effect, while leaving the cause untouched. Rather than attempting to change how society functions, we have to change our collective consciousness; thereby controlling our own reactions to our immediate environment. Unfortunately, very few people are even willing to entertain the possibility of changing anything about their way of life. The organizing principle of a society is its willingness and ability to make war, therefore some philosophers argue that human beings, especially men, are inherently violent. They argue that this violence is repressed in normal society requiring an "outlet" such as that provided by war. This is part of a philosophical theory known as displacement, in which someone transfers their grievances into bias and hatred against ethnic groups, nations or ideologies. In the context of systemic control, this is a valuable weapon. We have been programmed to expect and demand a quick fix in every aspect of our lives. Most people are unwilling to use their common sense regarding the causes of human conflict. Rather than face a complex ideological crisis, most people elect to retreat into unconscious (primitive) defense mechanisms. Why is it so easy for people to believe that Religion causes wars, yet somehow not recognize that all religions also have anti-war teachings as a part of their doctrine?

Many people find it reasonable that their particular religion somehow prohibits the tolerance and understanding of - or coexistence with other religions, yet at the same time find it unreasonable that their religion gives clear instructions on how to do that very thing. The denial of fear/hate based rationale also helps assuage any guilt of unethical knee-jerk reactions often displayed in the wake of fundamentalist rhetoric. Ideological diversity is both encouraged and frowned upon in society. The system has you either way. All that is needed to perpetuate systemic control is your compliance and continued emotional reactions to circumstances that may not even exist. Some believe that even the most insignificant ideological differences can trigger violent conflict in the same manner as religion. For example, the theory that Fascism's basic hatred of Communism contributed to the outbreak of war between Germany and the Soviet Union during the Second World War. So, I guess never mind that Hitler needed the oil from the caucus mountain region of Russia to continue his siege of Britain; and never mind that the Soviet (who two years earlier annexed more of Poland than Germany had) were comprised of the same groups of people whom most Germans blamed for causing their defeat in the First World War and vice versa; therefore neither side had any reason to trust the other or respect their boundaries. A pragmatic view of history based on raw material economics and conquest is more difficult to understand and accept than something as abstract as political ideology. Basically, people view the truth as being generally unpleasant. That is probably why objective truth is often revealed through various states of heightened consciousness or suffering. I sometimes find myself contemplating truth from a minimalist view of spirituality; in that I have confidence that the true nature of all things will be revealed as a matter of course. I put my trust in the spiritual rather than the material. Our greatest obstacles to seeking dual truth are materialism and emotion. Understanding why we place value on material possessions is the key to understanding all human conflict.

Some social activists argue that materialism is the supreme cause of social conflict and I agree with them 100%. I do not believe it is possible to separate mass coercion from so-called "personal responsibility" in terms of motivation, because your responsibility as a *person* is always to follow the masses. Corporate coercion is perpetual because it is systemic. Therefore, we have a <u>human</u> responsibility to act as an individual. Your motivation should begin with self; then continue through connecting with nature, family, community and culture. The sooner you realize that you are a slave to material consumption, the sooner you can experience an emotional, physical and spiritual awakening. The system has no interest in you being happy, healthy and productive. The US GNP actually reflects the number of citizens who are sick and dying. Chronic illness sustains the for-profit healthcare system. The health insurance industry creates Nine Hundred Billion dollars per year for large financial institutions. Mental and physical wellness is actually <u>bad</u> for the US economy.

You're just a dollar sign to the corporation. As a result, if you continually stay plugged-in, you can get away with making the same mistakes in life over and over again. But the moment you "unplug" yourself, you become public enemy. As far as the system is concerned, you can fall or jump off the hamster wheel as much as you want, as long as you get back on at some point and continue running. We are conditioned to believe that running on the wheel is natural and stopping for any reason is abnormal behavior. The masses are typically incapable of reason. Only the *individual* can truly reason. The masses move forward with mindless abandon. In this sense, large groups of realists and idealists are of equal value; <u>none</u>. Realists are perpetually jaded and the idealists are perpetually ineffectual. In order to reach full human potential you must create an individual archetype or model for objective reality as an ideological construct. Reality can therefore exist *beyond* the physical realm. Remember that being a great human being is much more important than being a good person.

Chapter III

I have been a writer since I have known how to write. In 1977 I wrote jokes using the words I knew how to spell. In 1980, I wrote an essay (my first) on the hostage crisis. Over the years as I became more prolific, observation and storytelling became my forte. At 16, I started writing reviews. I actually got paid on occasion. But I was an outsider. I had disdain for society's version of success. I eventually became a portrait of apathy and nihilism. I struggled with feelings of contempt for myself because I was still allowing the constraint of conformity to influence my work. No matter how controversial I was perceived, I still viewed myself as another cog on the wheel. That spring I left home for college and stepped off into the unknown with very little knowledge of how our society really functioned; and no actual desire to learn. I wasn't anti-social. I was outgoing, but my efforts to conform and assimilate were transparent. I typically spoke in a course, rough manner even though I had an extensive vocabulary. I got into fights on occasion, as the polarizing effect of my blunt, aloof personality seemed to intensify. But I still loved parties and social events just as I had as a child. And although I generally had a way with women, I also had a low opinion of them, especially as my contemporaries. This became very obvious to most women and I felt bad for not feeling more self-conscious about it. Eventually, out of respect for all the women in my life, I worked for several years to modify my ideas and behavior in regards to women, both professionally and personally. By my early twenties I felt that I had succeeded somewhat, in that my passive misogyny was only apparent during the course of a romantic relationship, which was a rare occurrence. I was a twenty-something playboy. I counted cards and pulled low-level cons, but I was never a gangster or a thug. I was smug and self-absorbed, but at the time I did not see a viable alternative. I tried so hard *not* to be the person everyone expected me to be, that I lost sight of who I was gradually becoming.

I was a popular cat on the scene, but the issues I raised and topics I wrote about were controversial, to say the least. On a lighter, more intellectual side, I read a lot. I enjoyed acquiring arcane knowledge. I read all the dialogues of Plato and everything by Joe Conrad. I was well versed in Brother Bill Shakespeare and I spent hours studying and analyzing the films of Stan Kubrick, Rome Polanski and Bob Altman. On a heavier, more introspective side, I felt by the laws the nature, no peace, justice or equality could *ever* be realized on this stolen land; by anyone, until the system is entirely crushed. I firmly believed with all my being that the corporation otherwise known as the United States and its' capitalist death machine of corporate fascism was fueled by the blood of the living and the bones of the dead. No matter what level of social consciousness you subscribe to, you have to admit that these topics are not generally regarded as pleasant dinner conversation. But I did not care about any of that. In my eyes, social acceptance was seen in the same light as failure. At the time, I still believed in right and wrong, although I didn't always draw an absolute distinction between them. I was living a dual existence; half the time I was focused, with direction and drive. The other half was taken up by bitterness, contempt and apathy. Art Schopenhauer believed that life was a reflection of one's will - and the will was an aimless, irrational and painful drive. However, he found that salvation, deliverance and escape from suffering as well as having sympathy for others could be attained through aesthetic contemplation. That makes sense to me. For years I read about Intelligent Design being proof of God's existence, but I saw no direct evidence of that theory as it related to my surroundings. But like many young writers my perspective was skewed. Before I learned to love transcendentalists, I thought they were selfish pricks; always mouthing off about how beautiful a lake was, as if they were the only ones who could see that. But I was dead wrong. Love of nature is not selfish – it's *selfless*, as there should be no separation between nature and the self. Nature should always be a reflection of self.

I began to study the Cathars and their philosophy of gnostic Christianity. I began to realize that we exist simultaneously on several planes of being. I finally began to realize who I was and started working toward who I wanted to be. It was a rough road and it took several years, but it was the only direction I could have followed in order to bring me to this point. I tried to learn about every aspect of who I was and who I was not. A unique writing style began to develop. Like everything else in the universe, it had two sides. On one side I had a tendency to supersaturate people with my angst, usually out of contempt. Little did anyone know at the time that "nerd snark" would actually be tony someday among hepcats. On the other side, I was very subtle but direct and sincere. This side of my style eventually spawned my polite condescension. I always wanted to appear urbane, but I made very little conscious effort to demonstrate those qualities. A literary critic once handed me a note that stated "rudeness becomes you". To which I later sincerely replied to him with a letter thanking him for the compliment. And I was dead serious. Despite my highly visible character contradictions, I still managed to get people to support me and my ideas. I began to develop a more universal pattern of speech to get my point across and things gradually came together. I didn't necessarily like who I was, but I was comfortable being me. In truth, chaos was my comforter. I held my "self" in contempt in order to socialize. I was an absolute wildcard. Even I had no idea what I was going to do from one moment to the next. Instead of choosing one thing and learning to master it, I chose a hundred things and learned to do them well enough to say with confidence that I knew how to do them. Personally I was mediocre, but professionally I was a genius. This type of complicity can easily lead to isolation. Most people are contemptuous of those who do whatever they want all the time. From their perspective it's difficult to trust someone who never fully commits to any one thing in particular. But that was and still is my essence. I couldn't change that about myself even if I wanted to.

My isolation eventually spawned a realization and then a breakthrough; enlightenment. By intentionally <u>not</u> mastering certain essential elements of being which guide me through life, I could actually learn to master life itself. My life and life and my existence do not serve the same purpose. One of my early quotes was "the middle of nowhere is actually the center of the universe". At the time I really had no idea what I meant by that. Today, I read it as the most profound and possibly most true statement I have ever made. Seeing the other side of things creates a better understanding. As I look back on my time spent "in the middle of nowhere", at first glance it appeared that I had learned very little about life. But looking more closely I realize that all human experiences contain lessons, even if seemingly insignificant at the time. I will always take with me a few lessons I learned while at my most nihilistic; when I was blinded by arrogance and steeped in the wretchedness of self-destruction. My life at age 17 seemed to crystallize into a perfect union of irony and poetic justice. But I knew somehow it was all a means to an end. I believe that human life has a singular meaning. I believe everyone and everything has a specific purpose, even if we never learn exactly what it is. I believe my purpose is to have an effect on another being in such a way that inspires them to carry on in pursuit of a revelation or awakening to a higher form of consciousness; a self-awareness. The problem is, I don't know when or how I will do this – or if it has already been done. I don't know who that someone is or what I will do or have done to affect them. It may have happened when I was 17 years old, or 5 years old, or ten minutes ago, or this morning. It may happen when and if I am 60 years old or it may happen on my last day on earth, or could have happened on my first. If I did something as a child to affect someone's life in order to serve their purpose then affect someone else and so on, what is the point of the rest of my life after my purpose has been fulfilled? The point is, we never know when our purpose is complete, which suggests that we have more than one – or our purpose is continual.

Because we never know when our purpose is realized; we should therefore live life as if the realization is eminent. That's how I always wanted to live. I was a very creative adolescent, but I was also a typical teenager. I had no longing for approval. I never fully committed to any single lifestyle format, because I saw it as a form of submission. I realize now this may seem ridiculous but at the time it made perfect sense. I enjoyed being on the fray. Although unpredictable, I have always been very methodical. This made me even more of an outsider than the off-beat sub culture I created. The condition now commonly referred to as OCD is what I used to call "ritual habit". When it rains, I wipe my feet on a rug an even number of times when entering a building. I systematically swipe lint off of my clothing and pat myself down to confirm my gear. I bathed a lot as a child. That was "me" time. Most of my friends had to be threatened into bathing. I never considered myself to be normal, whatever that is. I automatically rejected most things that were widely accepted. I tried to find deeper meaning in most situations. I focused on my personality contradictions rather than my social attributes. I secretly viewed most compliments as insults. I was contemptuous of how people instinctively focused on appearance rather than essence. I was naïve to the game. I couldn't see the matrix. Everyone is young once - and everyone does things at a young age they probably shouldn't have, but I spent too much time beating myself up over nothing. And because no one taught me otherwise, I constantly worried about things that I was powerless to control. That is no way for anyone to live, much less a child. That is exactly why now I have a hard time worrying about anything. This may sound completely apathetic (and possibly nihilistic), but I care almost nothing at all about things that occur outside of my ability to control them. At the same time, I care deeply about the human condition, on which I ultimately have no effect. My empathy and disdain for humanity are concurrently on a shallow, corporeal level and a deep ethereal level. But that doesn't affect my behavior, only my beliefs.

Aristotle's law of non-contradiction states that "One cannot say of something that it is - and that it is not, in the same respect at the same time." I care deeply about humankind in general, but I do not care about anyone or anything outside of my scope of influence or determination. I was an extremely giving and unselfish young man, yet I had an intense paranoia that I could be easily taken advantage of. Those traits don't mesh well at all. I had an enormous vocabulary, but I rarely chose to utilize it. I have always been brutally honest yet very polite. Some of these contrasts are much less apparent, but they all have equal influence on my character. I understand this now, but back then it was very confusing. It made me seem more complex than I actually was. Eventually, I began to develop coping mechanisms to deal with these contrasts. I had to "psych" myself into doing everyday things that should have probably been routine. I found myself putting on an act, sometimes unconsciously. I would let people get close enough to me to understand what I was all about, but not so close that they would actually begin to care about my wellbeing. Like most writers and comedians I used my talent to mask my insecurities. I was not confident, but I had confidence in my abilities. When I was 14 years old, my friends and I formed a band. It put everything else we did into context. Weekend basement sleepovers became recording sessions. Enthusiasm about girls and sports was relative to our new found artistic expression. We interwove sketch comedy and music, like an old-school variety show. We wrote and illustrated our own satirical magazine and let our friends read it, but we never published it; as it would then lose its esoteric value. We all thought that it would be cool to get some notoriety, but our primary motivation was to keep from being trapped in a 9-5 existence. I was no stranger to live performance. I sang competitively in what was called choral assembly and in solo performances from age 9 to age 12. I enjoyed performing, but I hated rehearsing. I always felt as if I was missing out on something, so I eventually gave up performance altogether.

I feel now that this was a major mistake, even though life experience and conventional logic teaches us that crucial life decisions are not typically made at age 12. By then I had developed a keen awareness of young ladies, so I had little time for voice training. In many ways it was probably for the best. My friend Angelo Moore once wrote "people got problems that they can't work out, so their sense cracks". I have had the same basic problem since I was ten. I have long since given up on working it out. I always have too many girlfriends (too many as in more than one). So I can only imagine the kind of shenanigans I would have gotten myself into as an unhinged, out-of-control teenage crooner with a knack for anti-social behavior. However, in my defense, the results are fairly similar; I make films instead regularly perform on stage in between causing trouble for the establishment. Our band was formed out of contempt for pop culture. My disdain for the mainstream produces a distinct type of neurosis, but not a psychosis. I was not ashamed of refusing to jump head-first into the rat race. Although I felt as if I could have been doing more with my life, I had absolutely no desire to do it, or even find out what it was. As a compromise, I tried in vain to return to my roots as a vocalist. But after going through puberty with no voice training whatsoever, I went from a decent tenor to a one-octave range baritone. My voice was gash and well-knackered from drinking, cigars, shouting on radio shows and hosting open mic night. I continued to play and write music, searching for a style that matched my expression. Although I was regarded as a natural poet and a decent musician, I'm a horrible songwriter. I could never find a confluence of medium in that respect. Somewhere in between my rock-steady phase and hard-bop phase, I managed to give my inner turmoil a voice by writing essays. I was searching for meaning strictly on impulse, afraid of what I might find. As a direct result of limited parental supervision and typical teenage rebelliousness, I became more narcissistic. This fueled my nonconformity and made me reserved and overly cautious; almost withdrawn in frustration.

At that moment, to quote the Jules Winfield character from *Pulp Fiction*, "I had what alcoholics refer to as a moment of clarity". I began to ask what life was all about; for everyone who had ever existed. I wanted to know "why". I was not at all concerned about "how". At night, I stood outside and gazed at the sky in complete silence. I understood ancient cultures' fascination with the stars. I felt a connection with them; a continual oneness. We're still here – and they're still here, so there must be a correlation. As a youth, because my parents were biblical scholars, I studied religious history and world religions such as Buddhism, Jainism, Zoroastrianism and Gnostic Christianity. I understood that enlightenment had something to do with suffering. Then, it hit me all at once.

We as human beings, no matter how enlightened and however convinced of God's existence and God's "plan"; may never fully understand what that plan is. Upon hearing this, most people instinctively ask "what about the bible"? To them I say, what about it? It's a good book. One of many written for similar purposes. Fundamentalists encourage us to believe that an arbitrary group of people selected the perfect amount of relevant information about God, which had been previously revealed to separate group of people (who were all dead by then) who then handed down all the most vitally important instructions on human behavior and life philosophy given to them by an omnipotent, benevolent being in order to create a long-winded, stuffy, condescending, overly-complex and often mistranslated book for the benefit all mankind. When I spell it out that way, it all seems like an internet scam. Fundamentalists are basically just annoying salesmen. But in the context of biblical *metaphor*, the answers are all there if you know where to look. I realize it's almost impossible to tell when I'm being serious, but right now I am being completely serious. I actually support an allegorical myth of God's existence. If I was an all-powerful being I would much rather do some magic tricks and hip a few like-minded folk to what's going down rather than show and tell everyone individually forever and ever.

If God told each and every one of us, at a particular moment, in a clear distinct voice, exactly "where it's at" so to speak, with no room for question or compromise, then what would be the point of life thereafter? To be fair, some people truly believe God has done that very thing. I am no position to argue with them and I now believe that the voice they are referring to is actually the voice of "self". We can't always hear it, or we don't always listen, but that voice always speaks with regard to our best interest. As for those who do not hear the voice in any way, shape or form, God must therefore be an unconscious enigma. Your purpose may be to accept, reject or ignore your feelings about what you think God is, just as someone else's purpose may be to instinctively act on what they believe to be the *will* of God. As a result of this dichotomy I began to overanalyze my spiritual catharsis. It seemed that I had merely traded confusion for frustration. I struggled to keep it together. As the days progressed, I began to feel resentment instead of relief. As it turns out, from a sociological perspective, ignorance *is* bliss. The more I discovered about the meaning of life, the more I realized that human existence in relation to the world around us, is enigmatic. By age 18, I understood why so many intellectuals and creative geniuses contemplated suicide. I had to keep reminding myself that there is no such thing as luck or coincidence. The law of probabilities is bound by a predetermined course of action. Everything is as it shall be; in a state of motion, growth and adaptation. When I finally allowed this to sink in, I felt instantly better about life's meaning and human purpose. I realized that spiritual enlightenment is a journey, not a destination. Through all of this, one aspect of my psyche remained intact. Revolutionary free thought is the most influential part of my character. I am in continual open rebellion, even potentially against rebellion itself. I scorned attachment so I could do anything I wanted, and in my solitude, I purposefully did nothing. For the next two years I did as little as possible in every aspect of my social and professional life. I wrote only for myself. A 'revival" of self.

The question is, if I didn't already know who I was, who would I be? I only became an idealistic version of that which I thought should be because I believed that I had no control over who I really was. But that presumption was false. My control exists as part of a predetermined outcome, as my "self" is the predetermining factor. The world is just a construct. It exists as part of a matrix. Matter exists in a physical sense because impulses from my unconscious mind make it so. When I die, the world as I know it goes away - so therefore from my perspective, it only exists as a transitory condition. The study of electromagnetic fields in relation to matter strengthens this theory. The "here and now" as confirmed by my senses is an ongoing estimate of homeostasis. Voices on the phone are just that, voices. Until we walk outside, there is no outside. All matter in existence may be a construct of collective unconsciousness or hive-mind programming. From this point of view, the universe is infinite darkness, with "self" acting as light. Everything outside of our knowledge and senses exists only as belief. In other words, nothing relevant to self exists until self-illumination. When that light goes out, so goes the world. Some researchers refer to this as the "God-Man theory", but I would label it the "animal-man" theory; unconcerned with truth - only concerned with reality. The LDS scripture called *Articles of Faith* states "As we are now, God once was, As God is now, we can become". Although critics of Mormonism consider this blasphemy, it is one of the few LDS teachings that clicked with me. Keep in mind that most religious teachings are contextual. This is difficult to explain to most folks, especially as neither a true believer nor a modern skeptic. My goal is to share and discuss philosophy with anyone who is interested. I accepted long ago that most people will never be interested. I'm fine with that. After high school I began writing and editing my own literary magazine by day and by night spinning records at all-ages nightclub shows and basement or garage parties. I was determined to upset everyone who blindly followed mediocrity.

My brash literary style caught the eye of a few magazine editors who invited me to contribute. I was a freelance syndicated columnist by age 20, of which I should have been proud; but pride was as much a stranger to me as fear, guilt or shame. I experienced feelings of pride in others but not in myself. My fate seemed so preordained. There was little time for self-reflection. The early 90's swept me into the Kingston Jamaica "Ragga"/Dancehall Reggae scene. Elements of the culture surrounded my being. I was so drawn to it, that I even began to speak in patois with a slight Jamaican accent. Like most young adults, I smoked ganja a few times, but I never achieved the desired effect, as described by those who smoked it consistently. I have some sort of "natural immunity" to the psychedelic effects of cannabis, but it helped ease the continual pain of tendinopathy. Luckily, I don't have immunity to *Red Stripe* lager with lime. When some of my friends asked me why I didn't have a spiritual objection to moderate beverage consumption, I informed them that beer was first brewed by Sumerian priests and later by Medieval Monks who messed around and added hops to it. All those cats are a keen swarm of eels in my book. You don't know better than them. At the time, I had possession of a fake ID, so I had been twenty-two since I was seventeen. I would forget how old I really was on a regular basis. I could never remember what age I had told someone previously, so I began saying "25" as a default. But that's how teenagers' minds work. Our brains weren't fully developed. Things didn't need to make sense to me. It just is what it is, even when it isn't. I completely separated the corporeal world from my spiritual self. I developed an "all or nothing" attitude in my work. I refused to accept mainstream writing gigs to advance my "career". Writing is not especially difficult for me. I could have easily written schmutz and dreck just to get by while searching for meaning on my off days, but for some reason that never occurred to me. I felt that if I became an unwilling part of a zeitgeist I would miss an opportunity to finally understand the meaning of existence once and for all.

I expected my life experiences to bring about a cathartic rebirth as an enlightened human being. I felt an overwhelming obligation to find out who I was supposed to be in an objective sense. My solitude had made me intensely myopic. My essays suddenly seemed more like manifestos. As an eco-anarchist, I never even thought of asserting myself as a commercially "credible" author. The fact of the matter is I never wanted to be another brick in the wall. I would get into a scrape here and there, and I did some things that I probably shouldn't have. But I always stuck to my guns, so to speak. By staying out of the limelight, I found out more about myself than I could have possibly imagined and I did it with hardly a shred of compromise. Of course I suffered, as we all do at some point. But that suffering eventually gave way to enlightenment. So let me hip you to what I learned in my first 5 years as a writer:

I learned that the purity of essence can be a tangible reality - and it can be found in many different forms. I learned that appearance is nothing more than a paradox illusion. The sum of all objects does *not* form a totality of being. Systemic society's version of truth *is* completely subjective. Risk and faith are invariably linked; and the greater the risk the stronger the faith. Business ethics do not exist but individual human ethic is an absolute necessity. Given my new-found Methodism, I did what I could to square things with myself; to go beyond myself whenever possible. In my mind, I had much to atone for; my idleness and egotism were eating away at my consciousness. I know that my purpose is to become a definitive version of my "self" but I still had a great deal of repressed anxiety. I was aware that I have to continuously perpetuate my principles and embody or personify them until my influence reaches the next potentially free spirit. But as I said before, there is no way to know when that is – or was. It may have already happened. It may happen tomorrow. There is no way to know for sure, yet I believe that it has or will happen as a part of my destiny. The circumstances under which we all make life decisions are the details of a much larger plan.

Destiny is a predetermined course of events. Purpose is a specific part of one's destiny. The future is predetermined, both for humanity and the individual, but along various interconnected paths. We don't fall asleep specifically to dream. Dreaming is merely a consequence of sleep, just as death is a consequence of life. There is an Islamic proverb, "those who do not fear death - do not die". Although I have no fear of death, I do have a great deal of respect for it. I wrote a term paper in college called *Death is the Meaning of Life.* At the time I felt that I had an unhealthy preoccupation with death. But since I have come to realize that my perception of death is ideal. I was never morbid or Gothic about it; I just embraced death as an essential part of my being, perhaps even the defining part. Life is after all, simply the characteristic state of organisms. Some biologists believe that a capacity for descent with modification is the only essential property of life. Despite that, as Billy Preston sang so eloquently, *all things must pass*.

Death is the end of vital functions in a biological sense, but death can also be figurative; as when modern physicists anthropomorphize natural occurrences to better understand or describe them, such as a "dead" star. I am often asked about my feelings on life after death. In my opinion, if no higher state of consciousness exists after passing from the material realm, the entire concept of life is utterly pointless. Why would we be allowed to live, on average only ¾ of a century but be dead forever and ever? It makes no sense. I believe that humans experience various planes of existence more than once, but not necessarily in a continuous cycle as some Eastern religions suggest. The word Samsara in Tibetan dialect means "continuous flow" and describes how the spirit is affected by Karma. The Buddha believed that a perception of reality and realization of truth completes the cycle, thus liberating the soul. Reincarnation is very attractive prima facie; as an ethical life determines graduated sentience. However this is a parable and not to be taken literally. It would mean that our beloved pets and most farm animals are just former human assholes.

Anyone who has met my pal Bosco (AKA Cool-Jerk) will tell you that he's a pretty cool cat for a dog, but he's also kind of a dick. I can't help but think that in a former life he was a politician or stockbroker or corporate executive. Maybe in this life he will work toward being reborn as a space-chimp or a dolphin, but I doubt it. He will probably come back as a goat or pig. He's definitely not going to make it back to humanity by chewing up my flip-flops and making love to the sofa. Unless that is the point of existence, in which case we are all going the wrong way. When I was a kid I embraced reincarnation as viable alternative to the ridiculous concepts of "heaven and hell". Like most teenagers, my entire perception of religious philosophy was clouded by the basic principles of dual philosophic reality. My admiration of Plato but disdain for Socrates was a hindrance to my understanding of the universe. Socrates believed that "before anyone can understand the world, they first need to understand themselves; and the only way to accomplish that is through rational thought." As a young writer, I was resistant to that idea, because I did not want to understand who I really was. I was happy with who I *thought* I was. Socrates never published or even wrote down any of his thoughts, but he had constant discussions with people around him. I was sore at him because I felt he was pretentious. He started conversations by asking a question, to which someone would volunteer an answer. He continued to ask questions until the issue was resolved or until someone admitted that they didn't know the answer. But Socrates didn't claim to know the answers either. He approached the issues critically and rationally. Unlike Socrates, Plato wrote down his philosophical theories, in the form of manuscripts. Plato's writings feature debates or "dialogs". Their central theme is the conflict between nature and convention; concerning the role of heredity and environment on human intelligence and personality - long before the modern "nature versus nurture" debate began during the time of Tommy Hobbes and John Locke. Plato wrote about the distinction between knowledge and belief.

According to Plato the main difference between them is the "nature of their objects"; knowledge is of eternal truths while true belief is of transitory, contingent truths. The most important thing I learned from both Plato and Socrates is that debate is healthy, no matter the subject; in almost every context. The ideal purpose of debate is to assist in problem solving, develop awareness or create different points of view. But debating to this end – in this capacity, no longer exists. Pure debate has been coopted by political and social debate; which is nothing more than a popularity contest or talent show. Since most modern argument positions are completely subjective, debate has become a platform used specifically to create a so-called consensus, which causes more problems than it solves. I'm not particularly interested in what most people feel is right or wrong, because most people are slaves to social conditioning. I don't need advice on how to capitulate to the system of control, thank you. I'm being forced to tap-dance. I refuse to take tap-dancing lessons. Ironically, most people reject my debate philosophy due to its simplicity.

My most common criticism is that I tend to oversimplify, as if that were possible. My personal philosophy of keeping life simple and accepting truth as authority is seen by most as uncompromising. Most people are willfully ignorant of their reality. I am willfully ignorant of systemic consensus. What people know – or think they know, is only of consequence to me as it relates to my wellbeing and environment. When I'm introduced or I introduce myself to "celebrities", they are sometimes taken aback when I ask their name. I'm not being pretentious. It's because I don't know who they are. Because I don't care. Money and fame do not impress me. I measure success and prosperity by inner peace and spiritual harmony, not by outward appearance and material possessions. I don't care how much you think you own, because your so-called possessions actually own you. You're compromising integrity to get them - and keep them. You are the slave. Material is the master.

The human condition requires cooperation, not competition, which only belongs in sport. Even then, it should be kept in the context of being "just a game". Sporting events have become a billion dollar amusement industry to keep you distracted from what is really happening. It's interesting that the winners thank Jesus for giving them the strength to crush their opponents while the losers blame themselves for not being good enough. It's a microcosm for what society has become. That's why sports and the military have become interconnected. The goal is to equate competition on every level with social prosperity and personal happiness. We are bombarded with messages of being bigger, stronger and faster in regards to physiology and consumer technology. We are forced to sign 2-year contracts to use technology that will be obsolete in six months. Human beings have become a virus on the living organism known as earth. Modern society is the disease.

The more complacent we become in our role as the pathogen, the more earth will continually destroy us in order to heal itself, to which it has every right. In modern capitalist society, technology is not used to improve the quality of human life; it is used to maintain the system of control. Most do not seek God to achieve inner peace or self-awareness, but as an escape from reality or desire to conform out of a childish fear of damnation. But the system always keeps the rationale in place. Control systems of money and religion have made humans into persons – and persons into corporations, while conditioning us to accept these circumstances with no alternative. Mark Twain once wrote "happiness and sanity are an impossible combination". If you remain as a slave to the system he is exactly right. Parents sometime agonize over wanting their children to grow up either happy *or* intelligent, as the two cannot coexist within the system. Psychologists, most of whom answer to corporations, try to sell people on the idea of life/work 'balance". But that is still capitulation. My point is that once you discover the *gnosis*, your mind is free. Life is not about finding yourself; it's about creating your "self".

I realize now that I am in a constant state of self-monitoring, while at the same time completely unfazed by people's reactions to who or what I am. I am postmodern by default. My idealistic "self" is my natural or innate sense of rebelliousness. I am commonly referred to as a minimalist. Every day of my life I compare my wants vs. my needs and my impulses vs. my instincts. I don't believe in over-analysis or over-simplification. Everything in an individuals' environment should be relatable and symbiotic to that individual - within context. However, patterns of learned social behavior and systems of control and/or manipulation have destroyed the symbiosis between humans and our immediate environment. Unlike some of my contemporaries, I do not feel that this destruction can ever be reversed on a large scale. Nor do I feel that the destruction is near an end. Ages, Eons and Eras come to an end, but there is no such thing as the end of the world – only an end of us. If the "world" (suffering and enlightenment) does not have an end, then it also had no beginning.

Modernity has become so arrogant that it does not occur to those who believe in "the end of the world" that we are the primary cause of our own destruction. Society has become a giant engine; regulated by control systems and fueled by our servitude. We are forced to automatically subscribe to man-made laws which confine us, rather than physical and natural law which frees us and improves the human condition. The laws of man should never ever take precedent over the laws of the nature, regardless of what God is or isn't; because the interpretation of law is subjective. If the choice is between following a set of rules that I may never fully understand created by someone or something greater than myself - or following a set of clearly defined rules created by humans who lack understanding of *self*, then I chose to have a free spirit instead of a slave mind. My participation in our system is based solely on my knowledge of the truth and my purpose in this system is to share that knowledge. My soul is therefore perpetually free and thus unaffected by the laws of man.

If everything happens for a reason, then there is no such thing as a random occurrence. If everything seems to be going well, then suddenly things are not so well, we are faced with sometimes enigmatic scenarios of action vs. reaction. But all of our choices have already been made. When we act on the resulting decisions that is an example of human behavior, not human nature. The outcome is predetermined, it just has yet to be revealed. Worrying about it is pointless. It is as it shall be. You're not being naïve if you think everything happens for a reason and there is no such thing as luck or coincidence. Most people have convinced themselves that all events are completely random and everything in existence is accidental. Still others believe that some occurrences are a matter of destiny yet still somehow effected by coincidence. You will not find any solutions through the belief (or disbelief) in "God". Because that is the easy part. The next step is more difficult.

When asked about belief in God, most people will simply answer yes or no. However, a small percentage who possess strong character will tell you what they believe is irrelevant. How we react and behave shapes our being. Although humans have lost symbiosis with our environment and therefore need to reestablish our relationship to nature, our inherent connection to all other matter in existence remains intact. All matter is related. Symbiosis exists outside biological interaction, into ethereal planes of being. It's odd that some people have a belief in luck, but also a belief in God, which makes no sense. Luck is a result of the law of probabilities, so by all means give credit to that which you worship and praise. Otherwise worship and prayer are nothing more than gambling. Brother Bonaparte once said "what the vulgar refer to as luck, is actually a characteristic of genius". He believed in being in the right place at the right time; the combination of skilled experience and character traits. But even if circumstances are ideal, no one is perfect. Everything is either an imperfect version of its ultimate form - or everything is exactly as it was meant to be. Both conclusions are valid – as a composite truth.

Individual reality is a perceptual illusion. When subjectivity creates a paradox, we should allow pragmatism to outweigh emotion in favor of higher consciousness. Luck and coincidence then becomes fate and destiny. So when do we reconcile our perception with the reality of our surroundings? Always. Never. Forever. This is the basis of human existence. We balance what is known with what is unknown, what we think and what we can prove, how we behave and how we feel, who we are and what we are - and what we will become once more. If everything happens as it is meant to happen, the result is a plan of existence. Life, death, creation, destruction, evolution (or adaptation) and enlightenment are all part of this plan; and part of each other. Life is the answer to existence as death is the answer to life. Some people fear death, which is seen by most to be a rational fear. I don't see it as being rational at all. Death is inevitable. If the "unknown" is the aspect of death that people are really afraid of, then that is an example of contextual rationality. We never really know what is going to happen to us from one moment to the next. We can fall down the stairs, get struck by lightning, or have some type of fit, etc. and so on. The finality of death as the cessation of life is what concerns people the most, because they believe that matter is the only thing that matters. I believe that physical death is simply a transition to another plane of being. Because all planes of being exist simultaneously and all matter in the universe is connected, spiritually we <u>never</u> die. Human bodies are just vehicles for the soul. I never view death as something bad or wrong because it happens to everyone. We miss those who have passed away and mourn our loss, but we also celebrate their transformation into a higher state of being. When I think about my death, a recurring theme always revolves around those few moments after I die, as in my "realization" of death. But that's probably not how it works, because in death the construct of time no longer exists. I wonder if death is anything like hypnagogia. Is it tranquil and serene or is it intentionally designed to be disorienting like international air travel?

I love the 70's-genre and noir films in which the hero utters a memorable and inspirational remark before dying in the arms of a dusty companion or a glamorous beauty. In those situations, the final words of the dying are usually that of absolute or ultimate truth, at least from their point of view. But why should people tell the truth because death is imminent? It seems to me like an ideal time to lie. If I knew I was dying, I would say something completely outlandish so everyone would go bananas trying to figure it out. And what if someone thinks they are going to die and they don't? It would be a tough break to make a full recovery and then have to do a bid in the joint because of a death-bed confession, which actually turned out to be a regular-bed confession. If ultimate truth is somehow related to death, shouldn't we consider that to be inspirational in some way? Most people seem willing to take secrets to their grave. The logic being that those who are potentially impacted by knowing said secrets would be much better off by never learning about them. That seems like a fair assessment of the type of dirt some people keep as life-long secrets. If you suddenly find out from your mother that your uncle is really your father, long after they have both have passed away, are you really better off knowing about it? I'm not sure anyone can effectively answer that, until or unless it happens to them. I suppose you would have to work something out with your sibling-cousins or "couslings". Here is the point; truth is motivational. When I began studying Gnosticism, a progressive pastor explained to me that there are two different audiences for speaking the truth about Christianity; free thinkers and "church folk". Some philosophers refer to the non-spiritual ideological motivation of free thinkers as "secular motivation". The word secular is derived from the Latin word "saeculum", which is an expression of time as one generation or century. Based on the Judaeo-Christian doctrine that God exists outside of time, medieval scholars used the term to indicate movement away from religious ideology toward a more worldly doctrine, bound by the constraints of time.

The term has since been extended and now applies to the absence of any and all religious doctrine. Motivation is a temporal, dynamic state that should never be confused with emotion. It is the initiation, direction, intensity and persistence of behavior. Simply put, motivation is having the will and encouragement to go out and do something your "self" has aspired to. Motivation takes different forms, but it is typically made up of the same set of principles. Motivation can either be temporary or continual. The way someone becomes motivated is a direct result of their personality, considered to be the permanent characteristics of an individual's state of being. Set in juxtaposition to motivation, emotion refers to temporal states which do not immediately (but do eventually) link to behavior, such as anger and fear. The term secular motivation appears most often in the study of minimalism. When I began this monologue, I wanted to find out if I was in fact a minimalist. I felt that I probably was, and I had a good idea about what it means, but there were looming questions that I could not set aside about how it relates to my character. When I began filming the documentary *Freedom vs. Liberty* in 2005, I discovered that because I don't have much, I don't need much; and as a result, I don't want much. This seemed to portray me as a minimalist, at least from my understanding of it. I began to realize that there are two major motivating factors in the minimalist's lifestyle; a secular motivation, such as that of the starving artist or environmentalist; and a spiritual motivation similar to that of a priest or monk. I felt that my motivation was at least partially secular, imbrued with spirituality. I feel that this is due at least in part, to the definitive yet esoteric nature of my spiritual beliefs. This is the basis of Gnosticism. This is the knowledge of "self". I feel strongly about the "Christos" and I also feel that most so-called Christians have no idea what Christianity is really about. That is not to say these people aren't intelligent, I just think that the vast majority who identify as such have completely missed the point. I can't blame them directly for this misunderstanding.

The system of religious control is in place to suppress the true meaning of Christianity. Any and all interpretations that do not conform to the current system are automatically rejected by the majority of church folk. Free thinking is a direct threat to the "church" establishment. Church-sanctioned interpretations must be kept on an infantile level, such as "good vs. evil", to perpetuate the systemic ideology. For example, the modern concept of being "saved" or accepting *the Lord* Jesus Christ as your "personal savior" takes infantile concepts to new heights. Even though the term "personal savior" makes absolutely no sense and Jesus never specifically asked or told anyone to "accept" him, while living or dead - for any reason, much less as a necessity for salvation, and even though Paul (who never actually speaks of Jesus as a human being) says "Christ died for our sins, according to the *scriptures*", he never cites any of those scriptures in particular. Most so-called Christians will tell you that unless you accept a narrow set of lifestyle criteria exactly the way they present it, then you are somehow <u>not</u> one of those for whom Christ supposedly died, even though Paul does not make that distinction. In fact, none of the four gospel writers specifically mention Christ dying for our sins. Seems like an important detail to mention, but they don't. Even Paul himself referred to unsourced material. That entire concept could be one of Paul's own creation. That's fine with me. I like Paul. I like him even more when he is being criticized by church folk. Similarly, any belief in hell, or being condemned to hell, is equally infantile if not more so. Deuteronomy 31:8 says The Lord *your* God will NEVER leave or forsake you. He doesn't say except. He doesn't say unless. He doesn't say however. He said <u>never</u>. And I'm guessing that hell would be pretty damn forsaken. So if you believe in hell, either you don't know what the word "never" means, or you think God was jerking everybody around, in which case what's the point? If you can't – or refuse to understand that the bible is written as a cryptic, contextual metaphor, then you may want to find a different book to pattern your life after.

I don't necessarily recommend the Koran or Talmud either, as they follow the same patterns in a different format. Try *the Odyssey*. It's pretty good, or maybe *Animal Farm* or *What Color is your Parachute?* How about *Catcher in the Rye*, or *Dr. No*? They're all great suggestions really, but don't just take my word for it (queue the *Reading Rainbow* star-wipe). And don't get mad at me because you don't understand how literature works. If you're reading this book, you must be into books, because there is a high probability that this book will never become a motion picture. And if you're into books you should already understand context and metaphor. The bottom line on Christos or Christ is unchanged. It doesn't matter if he was an actual man, or an ethereal being, or one of the "Sons of God", or a composite literary character, or a Roman construct to promote change and further social control through a church-based system of laws. Christ could have been all of those things combined or none of them at all. The important lessons to learn and remember are love, compassion, creativity, forgiveness, kindness, peace, humility, patience, tolerance, sacrifice and wisdom. Christos as "oil or anointed", whatever or whomever that is or may have been at one time, echo my strongest convictions; love for humanity and respect for nature. My favorite prayer is that of St. Francis. It cryptically describes the symbiosis that the human self should have with nature. The personification of nature as our mother is appropriate as a nurturing life-giving entity. Nature can be harsh on occasion, but is often synonymous with peace and tranquility. I find it interesting that modern so-called Christians devote themselves to those who are dedicated to war and marginalize those who are dedicated to peace. That's because there is no money to be made in peace. Modern Christianity, along with the rest of organized religion has become inextricably linked to the monetary system, which thrives on continual warfare. Tertullian said it best, "only <u>without</u> the sword can the Christian wage war: for the Lord has *abolished* the sword." Those who wage war are not following the price of peace.

Only a pacifist can personify the concept of Christianity, as the "Christos" personifies peace. If most so-called Christians were more like Christ, they would all worship and praise in unity. But they do not. A basic idea of peace and love has been co-opted by the Roman Empire (which never fell) and carved into a thousand pieces after a successful rebellion. There are literally thousands of denominations in Protestantism alone. In some countries people kill and die over the distinctions. The Gnostics believed that all Christians should worship as a part of one large group; in a leaderless, equal and autonomous society. Christians should ideally congregate to worship and praise <u>outside</u> of the church system, as the word "church" is derived from the name of the Greek Goddess "Circe", daughter of Hyperion, the Sun deity. She was the goddess of magic; an enchantress who treacherously seduced people into her lair to cast spells on them, turning them into animals, making them more easily controllable. Her lair was known as the "Circus". In fact, the word church does not even appear in the bible. The Greeks used the word "Ecclesia" which simply means gathering or assembly. Most pop-culture intellectuals and biblical scholars completely misunderstand both the literal meaning and sub-text of ancient Greek. The word Genesis for example, means origin, source or beginning, but it also means reproduction, formulation and propagation; which means there was some form of existence prior to Genesis. Ancient Greece was a conglomerate of many cultures, languages and traditions. They "borrowed" (or more accurately co-opted) ideas and practices in several aspects of art, science, economics and philosophy. My point is that as an adult, you must think and act on your own accord. Question everything. Gnostic cultures such as the Cathars understood that we are not bound to this physical realm to be slaves of this world. The divine "spark" within us is proof that we are beings of a higher realm. So if you cannot or will not accept the peace, love and pacifism shared by your *redeemer*, then your entire concept of redemption is wrong.

Chapter IV

When an elderly person gets really close to me physically, I instinctively want to hug them. Sometimes when I'm talking to an old lady in a retail store or at a bank, I imagine myself caressing her delicate shoulders while she reminisces about 10 cent pies and motor vehicles you have to hand-crank to get started. Shaking hands with a really old fella is meaningful to me. I have respect for advanced age, even though it gives me the creeps. Sure, it feels like gripping a flaccid skin-bag full of clothespins, but that's not the point. That handshake is a poignant reminder of inevitability; a glimpse of an unavoidable future. I have always believed that the certainty of death would influence people to be less narcissistic, but instead I think it does just the opposite, aided by a relentless campaign of social conditioning. In the 1920's, the term "politically correct" was used by socialists as a guideline for the party platform. By the late 1980's the idiom was co-opted by conservative politicians to summarize all their fears of what they now call "multiculturalism". In my opinion, all politicians are scumbag criminals, equivocation or not, but I catch the drift. Idiomatic speech should be Omni-cultural, but it isn't.

When I mention someone who is fat, and I describe them as being "fat", in some people's mind I am a total jerk, even though that is the proper medical term. Having too many fat cells essentially means you're fat. In my mind, it isn't an insult at all. For example, my head and/or face is oval in appearance. It is what it is. If someone points that out I don't go home and cry about it, mostly because I can't do anything to change it. So my deliberate use of the word fat is only offensive because we're conditioned to become offended. And I wouldn't use the word overweight, because that may not even make sense. I don't know how much people are supposed to weigh. I'm not a nutritionist. I was always discouraged by my parents from using that type of curt, descriptive language. They assured me that I was probably going to hurt someone's feelings.

I understand where they are coming from, but it is hard for me to empathize on that level because I am detached from feelings of guilt. It's extremely difficult to feel guilty when I don't believe the things I'm doing are "wrong". I don't really even believe in collective right and wrong or good and evil. I understand negative and positive, ebb and flow, yin and yang; energy and ethic. In any case, I would not just walk up to someone and call them fat; I'm not a child, or a Russian woman. But if you're fat and you ask me if you're fat, I will say yes, because it is in context and no harm is intended. So when you ask me if I know some guy, and I reply, "oh yeah, he's about yay tall, kind of fat, etc." to which you turn up your nose, it's *your* problem. I'm not concerned with folks getting offended on someone else's behalf. Otherwise I would never be able to write comedy. I'm aware that my honesty in polite condescension causes folk to get their knickers in a knot. Once, while in Atlantic City, I barked at a row of hoes outside Caesars, yelling "how much for the big one, she's super cute?" Don't y'all know she got all sore at me? Seriously? For reals? For that? That was so tame compared to what I could have said. And why is she getting offended anyway? She's already a hooker. Dignity is not an element in that equation. She got so fresh about it that she went straight away and told her pimp on me. But he was just as confused about it as I was. He wouldn't even get out of the Cadillac. I couldn't understand why she was more upset at being called "big" than she was at being a prostitute in general. She already knows what she looks like. But that's how my arrogance works. I admit to being arrogant. But I am not *vain*. Vanity in men is extremely repulsive to me. In my experience, vain men can't be trusted. It's fair to say that social conditioning has influenced my point of view. Human males, for example, are considered less beautiful than females, but for most other species, the opposite is true. Look at a peacock compared to a peahen or a male lion compared to a female. His mane is symbolic, as if it were some kind of crowning feature. Set in juxtaposition, the human male is bland.

This wasn't an accident. It was intelligent design. Charlie Darwin's minions are getting squirmy now, so let me admit that inherent human attraction is based on perceived reproductive capability; taut muscles, big ole' behind, etc. The aesthetic inequalities between women and men should be embraced. Not better or worse, just different. I would never want to be "the pretty one" in a relationship. If you are a woman, and I'm prettier than you are, then you may have some issues that require attention. However, attractiveness is subjective. People like what they like, especially women. Everyone pre-judges, but not everyone will admit that. Looks are not that important to me because I don't judge people based on societies' standards. I created my own. Personability, intelligence and hygiene are more important to me than looks, no matter who you are, or think you are, because that's what works for me. Sure, I like attractive women, if they're nice with a great attitude. But if you treat folk like dirt, I wouldn't care if you're Miss America. To me you're just Miss American skank.

The tricky part is that you cannot measure concepts like vanity and arrogance by their textbook definition alone. They must be measured in context by their intrinsic value to the individual. Greed might be seen as ambition. Vanity could just be a high self-opinion. Arrogance could be viewed as confidence and so on. Philosophers and psychiatrists refer to this as selectivism. In almost all social situations, I am a complete anti-idealist. I neither accept nor reject concepts in their entirety. Instead, I seem to embrace certain particulars in order to justify my behavioral patterns to myself. I see both my arrogance and my awareness of it as a necessity. Perhaps another man's vanity is just as much of a necessity to him. If that is the case, then my distrust of such men is based partially on the self-reference criteria, which makes more sense. In regards to self-consciousness I am in the unique position of not being concerned with the opinions of others but extremely concerned with my self-opinion. Unlike most people, I am only self-conscious when I'm alone.

According to most psychologists' theories, this means that I am highly introspective. Sig Freud referred to this as "the bathtub self". Maybe that's why my bath time was important to me as a child. When I am by myself I am extremely cognizant of my being which includes my appearance. My appearance to "whom" however seems to be the very basis of my introspective thoughts. I am one being, but I am more than one existent. I am I, and I am also me - as well as myself. My concept of "self" is known in psychology as the "observing ego". Suddenly "talking to yourself" doesn't seem so strange does it? It also makes more sense than "thinking aloud" which makes no sense at all. I still seem to present a slight contradiction in that I have complete self-awareness without being concerned about the judgments of others. I constantly visualize an idealistic version of myself and my self-awareness is based solely on that visualization.

You can't have self-awakening without self-awareness and vice versa. I'm considered to be an idealist of a highly esoteric and arcane nature, but I'm not. I don't really need to justify myself to myself, but I do feel that I should always prove myself worthy in my own eyes. I appreciate critique, but I am not particularly concerned with most people's opinion of me. I don't feel that I need to justify that either, but I can explain where it comes from. Since I was a child, I have been creating a mental state of inherent resistance to social conformity. I have a default setting in my brain that causes me to "go my own way" on several key principles and concepts of sociology, interpersonal relationships and intercultural communication. I have contempt for the mainstream, but I'm not a reclusive weirdo. I'm social, outgoing and friendly. Yet I don't frown on those who build a house in the middle of the woods without tools and eat whatever they can gather or kill. For the record, I could do that if I wanted to. Straights up. Don't let the smooth taste fool you. I'm tough and deceptively fast, like a big mountain cat. You won't know where I am until it's already too late. You can't tame the wildcat.

I have always had an innate sense of autonomy or complete individuality. Even if I have a few things in common with a group, my own spin is in effect. My appearance, my behavior, my speech, my attitude - all uniquely individual, yet tailored as much as possible in order to meet the minimum social requirements (i.e. the basic criteria for human interaction). I'm not exactly opposed to shock value in getting my point across, but I am averse to flamboyancy outside the context of humor. It's just not my style. When someone is highly obtrusive in daily behavior and/or appearance, they are seeking the attention and approval of others. I don't need that. My goal is to easily interact socially. If my clothes are clean and they fit me well, I'm not interested in fashion. My style is just a reflection of my public persona, unless of course I am working; in which case I have no regard for my appearance whatsoever. My contempt for work fashion is fairly obvious. To some, it may seem selfish but from a minimalist perspective it's actually selfless. My self-awareness extends to inanimate objects in my environment and affects them as well. When I was six years old, my favorite toy was actually a big safety pin whom I named Charlie. I had plenty of toys, but I didn't like them as much. He was one of those big-ass fabric safety pins my Grandmother used to pin heavy drapes and upholstery together. He was my best friend. He was shiny and strong. Most of all he had a purpose in life. I admired the expediency in which he exacted revenge upon our adversaries. On occasion, I would accidentally leave him stuck to a towel that I had been wearing as a cape and my Mom would unknowingly throw him into the washer and dryer. Many times my older sisters would get out of the shower and reach for a towel expecting a warm, linen-fresh feeling of comfort; but instead get poked in the ass-cheek or mildly branded like a cow or sometimes both. Charlie didn't understand that he was hot and sharp, as he hadn't submitted to the laundry process voluntarily. My sisters would scream and yell threats at the top of their lungs before asking why someone would do such a thing.

"Why indeed" I said to myself while hiding in the clothes hamper and stroking my imaginary chin beard. Oh, how they conspired against us. On one occasion even going so far as to throw Charlie onto a lawn of high grass near a weed-wild garden. Although it appeared that there would be no hope of rescue for Charlie, little did they know or appreciate the bond between Charlie and Neutron-Man. (That's what I called myself at age six although I had no idea what a neutron was or what it did.) I walked out onto a sea of green, as defiant as I was determined. Eventually I noticed a "glint" among the weeds. It was Charlie's SOS signal. After 20 minutes of combing through the grass on my hands and knees like a badger and getting all scratched up and bitten by various yard critters, I found Charlie, picked him up and stared at him through the haze of my teary eyes. As I carried him back inside I put him safely in my pocket and my tears suddenly turned to laughter.

I could sense that Charlie felt my enthusiasm and we shared a laugh at the absurdity of our downfall. Yet our overconfidence was soon to become our biggest weakness. A few weeks later at my grandparents' house I was taking a bath, careful not to let Charlie the safety pin out of my site, because in those days as I recall, treachery was everywhere. Despite this fact I became unusually careless. Somewhere between the 2nd and 3rd verse of the song "groove line" by *Heatwave*, Charlie slipped silently into the bathwater. When it was time for me to get out, my Grandmother gave me a towel and drained the tub. As I went to retrieve Charlie and could not find him, concern turned to panic as the tub continued to empty with no Charlie in sight. The drain in that tub was one of those wide old-fashioned drains and only God knows what else it had devoured over the years. I was extremely upset. I didn't think I would ever calm down. My Grandmother assured me that my Grandfather would retrieve Charlie from the drain and not to worry about it. Although I did not believe her, I had no choice but to take her word for it.

The next morning during my ritual of breakfast cereal and television, my Grandfather walked in the room and pulled a large safety pin from his pocket. "Here go your pin, boy," he said. I took it from him and said 'thank you" in a child's faint morning voice. I put it in my pocket and kept watching television. Although I was meant to think it was Charlie, I knew that it wasn't. I mean, you can't just replace someone's best friend without them noticing. But I wasn't upset in the least. Mostly because I knew how much it agitated my Grandfather to wake up early on a Saturday morning and drive to the fabric store to get a 5-cent safety pin. That is also why I thanked him for it. My obscure compulsions shouldn't have been his problem, or anyone else's. Non-acceptance is the risk, and often the result of creating your unique self. As an adult you must eventually weigh the risk versus the reward.

There is a constant conflict between our unconscious impulses and media mind control. Behavior resulting from an unconscious thought process which is contrary to the mainstream is usually taken as a sign of abnormality. I have a mild yet distinct form of OCD which practically undetectable. On close inspection, my unconscious, methodical behaviors may seem irrational, but that's fine with me. The life-long social conditioning that we endure has but one aim, to destroy our inherent human impulses in favor of conformity at every level. I have a metaphysical need or as psychologists refer to it, a "compulsion" to do things in a rhythmic pattern, though not necessarily always a continual or repeating one. I also arrange certain – but not all objects in my personal environment to form a grid pattern. Most items in close proximity are either parallel or perpendicular. The only intersecting lines of sight or horizon are those of 90 degrees. Currently on my desk I have a stapler, a tape dispenser and a baseball in a perfect right angle with a sports-bottle, coffee mug and mechanical pencil set. But there is also a pile of bolts in no particular order or pattern at all. It's because I'm not concerned about the bolts.

The bolts are in a transient state. The other objects, for the most part, are static. When I was a small child, my parents called me "the little general" because I lined up my toys, books and baseball cards as if they were an army of objects sent to attack or waiting to defend. To this day, I am extremely methodical. I speak in short, staccato phrases while telling a story or a joke, regardless of the subject matter, yet conversationally my speech is very fluid. It is as if two different people are saying the same thing in a different way. It's called an unconscious pattern of behavior. It isn't right or wrong, it just is what it is. Most people experience it in some form, yet some may never notice it or will refuse to acknowledge it. Those who realize their unconscious compulsive behavior sometimes feel immediately self-conscious about it and try to stop what they are doing, just like changing an unpleasant topic in conversation. But very few take steps to understand their unconscious tendencies. We are socially conditioned to avoid asking philosophical questions about behavior.

Self-consciousness, like everything else, has a negative and a positive aspect. It's difficult for me to remember what public self-consciousness feels like. Sometimes at parties or social occasions I actually pretend to be a little self-conscious in order to mingle more effectively. But maybe that is my version of humility. Admittedly, I only pretend for selfish reasons. I am attracted to women who have strong opinions about men's appearance. In this instance I am demonstrating my willingness to improve while simultaneously asking for valued input, regardless of whether I value that opinion. It is an attempt to demonstrate humility and preempt awkward opinion, although it does not always seem genuine. In any case, it's not about my social interaction strategies; it's about reflecting my patterns of unconscious behavior by making a positive impression through personal interaction, I am collecting theoretical ammunition as it were - to be used at some point in the future. If my intent is ever taken by someone to be some type of self-correction, then so much the better.

My goal in social interaction is not deception or dominance but to demonstrate the effect of unconscious influences on the observing ego. This effect is completely individualized by our obsessive compulsions yet is synthesized into a common thread by being part of a bigger picture. The mathematic patterns that surround us in nature directly influence our individual patterns of behavior; and as a matter of course, we in turn influence our environment. This is the basis of symbiosis from a human's point of view. The more you become familiar with your unconscious patterns, the more you can learn to translate them into personal characteristics. I sometimes have such awareness of my impulses that I can analyze people's reactions to them as they occur. It is as if I am looking at myself from a third-person perspective. I can recognize a meaningful conversation between secure adults when they notice each others impulses yet have no reaction to them. Maybe their lack of reaction is actually part of a strong social need; "comfortability" in response to something they don't understand or approve of. That could be why so many people watch presidential addresses on television.

Voyeurs for example, are sometimes not so much aroused by invasion of privacy but intoxicated by an "observation of routine", which can be very hypnotic. This is a typical example of how social conditioning is designed to confuse us. Voyeurism is frowned upon by most of society yet "reality" television shows are among the highest rated. Only the stigma of social non-conformity separates the observer from the peeping-tom and the researcher from the damn weirdo. Case in point, it is acceptable in our culture to watch monkeys and other animals bonk each other on cable television, but it is *not* acceptable to watch the fat couple next door get it on through a gap in the blinds. Why is that? The sheer mechanics of fat intercourse is way more interesting than monkey lovemaking, which offers almost no variety in comparison. In addition, the stigma somehow doesn't apply to both parties; it only applies to the observer. Exhibitionists often get a free pass from society.

The fat couple next door could easily close the blinds; but it's obvious that they *want* someone to watch. Unlike monkeys, who usually have to live in the woods or a habitat, people can easily have sex in a private setting. Perhaps Circus performing or Air Force monkeys have a slightly higher expectation of privacy, but your run-of-the-mill zoo monkeys will generally get busy wherever they happen to be. Ironically, monkeys seem to be evolving into creatures capable of forming "human-like" societies. Chuck Darwin's ghost is probably all like "Boom! I told y'all! Now bitch what?" Yet we seem to be getting mixed results from a century and a half of monkey research. Recent primate studies indicate that chimps are developing primitive weapons. They're fashioning spears for hunting, to impale small mammals living inside trees. We should probably be concerned about that, but we claim apathy as a basic right of being human. Putting things out of our mind through rationalization is par for the proverbial course.

We seem to have an instinctive delusion about letting things follow a "natural" plan of action by removing ourselves entirely from certain situations. I am convinced that we are made to feel guilty by social influence. Inherently, humans have no guilt. "People" develop guilt, human beings do not. And isn't it amazing what people will do to absolve themselves of guilt. Some people routinely go out of their way to give money to homeless people. Wouldn't it be better to examine the system that created their condition? Or better yet, ask why this problem exists in a so-called advanced society? Why is it perfectly reasonable that your phone recognizes biometrics yet many of your fellow humans are sleeping on the street? For the record, I don't give them money. But that's mostly because I don't carry any. Contributing to establishment pan-handling is completely pointless. It's like tossing sand onto a beach. I give food, clothing and support, which is more valuable than loose change. I'm almost envious of them. They're 100% unplugged from the system. Spiritually they are better off.

Sometimes I volunteer at community centers and donate clothing and food to local organizations. At times I work beside people who have been *forced* to volunteer. Our society actually views "community service" as a punishment. My neighborhood homeless man is mentally ill, often having grand karate battles against teams of invisible ninjas. When he's lucid, and probably "on the meds", he is a super nice guy. When he's not, I advise you not to mess with him under any circumstance. In either case, I never give him money. Because neither one of us are a part of the Rumple Geist. The truth is that he doesn't <u>need</u> money. He understands perfectly well that the world cannot provide a solution, because the world is part of the problem. When you see a man or woman living on the street, and he or she is wiping windshields, pushing a cart, yelling at invisible ninjas, etc., regardless of your instant perception of them as a junkie or a drunk or being mentally unstable, stop for a moment and ask yourself a very simple question; what are they going to do with pocket change? Money usually exacerbates depravity in the human condition. So, if I give my free street comrade's excess change and 10-20 other people do the same thing, that's just enough to get them loaded on poisonous fortified wine or at best, a few small portions of fast food. Alternately, rather than ignoring them, some feel the need to be indignant and judgmental; accustomed to using their centrism and privilege as a weapon of passive aggression. This is most evident in how the petty bourgeois react to the physically and mentally challenged. As a result, the challenged often have a particular insight into the righteous indignation of others because they develop strength of character. They are forced to watch non-challenged assholes walk through their pitiful, miserable lives, bitching and complaining about meaningless nonsense. So many people take so much for granted. I met someone once who had no arms and did everything with his feet. I never heard him complain. He could play the banjo…with his feet! Most of you thankless jackasses can't even play the banjo with your hands.

This guy drove to and from work every day with his feet. He stepped on the specialized pedals with one foot and steered with the other. 1950's Jazz drummers probably couldn't even do that. The pedals are over-sized and on the dashboard, but still. People are conditioned to be egocentric and at the same time naive. The social ideal is for amputees to wear uncomfortable prosthetic limbs rather than have a sleeve or pant leg pinned-up, because it triggers bourgeois sensibilities and destroys their image of conformity. It sometimes makes folk feel so bad that they can't finish their 5 dollar cup of coffee. Not everyone deserves this admonishment. But life is not about what you deserve. It's about what you give, what you take and how you deal with all of it. Understanding the importance of universal law and how you relate to it is vital to your existence. You must mature past infantile concepts of good and evil or right and wrong. Understand how human energy works and learn to make it work for you.

Regardless of how someone treats you, if you are courteous and polite in response you have done your part. Remember, people who desire constant conflict actually hate themselves. They are angry at the world for being born into it and will not listen to reason. Do not weigh yourself down with someone else's stupidity. Keep it together. You're better than that. If your behavior can inspire someone to do something positive the impact is eventually felt by everyone. We have all done things that we shouldn't have done. The most important thing is to keep moving forward. Understand that no one is perfect and there are no perfect solutions to common problems. Sometimes you must let your conscience be your guide. At some point, you have to trust your instincts. Learn the difference between instinct and impulse. Allow your "self" to guide you. Knowledge of self is the bridge between the physical and spiritual planes of being. Shape your character by improving your environment. Transfer negative energy objects into something worthwhile. Your reaction to your environment will always be reflected in your behavior.

Most 19th Century modernists did not understand the importance of human behavior or that humans are almost entirely reactionary. Therefore they concluded that humans are inherently violent. They believed the so-called "human condition" contained a predisposition toward violence. However, they did not factor in the socioeconomic effects of the industrial revolution and capitalist imperialism. Apathy in the face of duplicity is our greatest failure. Modern society's obsession with materialism is fueled by mass media and our consumption is driven by fear. Smug indolence and habitual greed will be the memoriam of this decaying system. The US Corporation has an undeserved superiority complex (soon to be shattered in North Africa and the Middle East) despite their obvious fear of and contempt for the Russian & Chinese. The US has the temerity to call its sports champions "World Champions" (Their rationale is that some professional athletes in the US are occasionally of international origin). This traditional sense of vanity should be offset by collective neurosis of modernity, but instead it's strengthened by it. Materialism necessitates possession, the root cause of conflict.

Philosophic materialism states that the only thing that truly exists is matter and all things are composed of material; therefore all phenomena are the result of material interactions, i.e. "matter is all that matters". Economic materialism reflects how people choose to spend money and time. A materialistic person collects material goods as a top priority. In other words, a materialist is a person in pursuit of wealth and luxury. Ironically, certain forms of considered and realistic materialism can lead to economic behaviors supporting a sustainable community. Thrift shops and garage sales for example, permit moderate materialism with very little social or environmental impact. Engaging in community commerce is often labeled "hipster" behavior; privately appreciated but publicly ridiculed. Why should you care where I get my meager belongings? One time I traded a bag of food with a vagrant for his tennis sweater. (He didn't need it. It was warm outside.)

I carried it home on a stick and washed it outside in a bucket under the spigot. Everywhere I went that fall people complimented me on how fly that sweater was. When people asked me where I got it, I would usually say it was a gift. But I really didn't care where it came from. It served a purpose. Consumption may not always be conspicuous; but it is typically driven by insecurity and self-consciousness. You can escape the trappings of materialism by understanding your life force, or spiritual energy. You will begin to realize that less is actually more. The constant accumulation of material goods creates an imbalance between our body and spirit. In other words, to be yourself, you must first know yourself. I no longer believe in labels. My system of values and spiritual beliefs could be defined as anything from agnosticism to gnostic anarchism (the belief that there is no higher authority than god/universe/self) to minimalist, to postmodernist, to existentialist. What it's called is not important. Those who seek the truth cannot logically discard any ideas that may help them find it.

In researching materialism and possession I often find myself embroiled in the history of religion. In particular Christianity; or at least what is considered to be Christianity by most folk. My prejudices about the common misconceptions and misinterpretations of Christianity have nothing to do with how I feel about spirituality in general. I keep "church folk" at arm's length intellectually and within walking distance philosophically, but I do not reject them. Materialism and Christianity have historically been at odds due on one hand to anti-materialist passages in Christian scripture; and on the other to denial by most materialist philosophers of the spiritual realities fundamental to the origins of the faith. However, the two are not always viewed as being in opposition. A concept known as Christian Materialism emerged from early fundamentalist movements in the late 20th century, in a takeover that went largely unnoticed outside the religious community. It eventually became crucial for the church to develop a new mechanism that closely paralleled materialism.

The supposed goal of the resulting movement was to reverse what they saw as the social decline that had accompanied the rise of individualism and the breakdown of "traditional" communities. To accomplish this, spirituality was abandoned (or sacrificed) as Christian idealism was becoming unpopular. Christian Materialism is used by some as a critical assessment of many modern American churches to adopt aspects of mainstream American material culture; A trend typified by the popularity of religious-themed material goods such as tee-shirts, wristbands and bumper stickers. The question that arises among spiritualists in response is why would anyone need material possessions to define or strengthen their beliefs? A better question is; why do your beliefs require any level of economic consumption at all? Perhaps that is the actual goal of Christian Materialism, the "possession" of so-called salvation. There's no difference between the idolatry of early Roman church who sold salvation to the lecherous wealthy and the idolatry practiced by those who give money to wealthy TV preachers in acceptance of their "personal savior". If you think salvation is a personal matter then your entire concept of salvation is misguided. An Eastern Orthodox monk at Simonopetra when asked if Jesus Christ was his personal savior said "No. I like to share him". A reasoning of the faith supersedes your particular rationale for belief. The set of beliefs that I accept and practice are a reflection of my mind and spirit. I don't owe anyone an explanation, but am happy to provide one. No human is spiritually greater any other. If you are fully in tune with universe, you must still exist on this plane of being. The Great Spirit as well as ethereal beings of higher consciousness are not bound by this plane. As they transcend human understanding and they are under no obligation to prove their existence. Jordan Maxwell once said "You can't make god do something he doesn't want to do - and whatever he decides to do, you can't stop him, so it's best to just go with the flow". My knowledge of the Great Spirit is based on belief, but my belief in the Great Spirit is based on knowledge.

Likewise, my belief that time and space are human constructs is based on my knowledge - my knowledge is not based on belief. My beliefs have almost nothing to do with my behavior. I don't make a distinction between behavior and intent. My intent is to encourage everyone to think before they speak, reason before they react and combine intuition with common sense. The reality of our surroundings is not absolute. There is a difference between acting on impulse and acting on instinct. You must take time to discover who you really are, so you can be comfortable with yourself and those around you. Accepting a sense of individuality as a part of social interaction is important to building unique character. When I was a deejay, I used to spin redacted sides or "white label" records with no title, just a number or phrase written in marker. This was to prevent rival DJs from biting my set as well as force everyone at the party to buy my mix tape straights up. I spent days on end developing my style. I didn't want to sound like any other DJ, but in order to get booked I had to conform. For a few years I vacillated between playing in a band and spinning vinyl.

I wanted always to be an artist, to create rather than consume, but I felt that I could be more influential working with multiple styles interchangeably. There were not many bands that could do that, or would want to. I was gradually building a reputation for not playing to the crowd. I read a review of myself in a local paper about how I managed to break the format I was supposed to be spinning in order to drop beats that no one had heard of. Mainstream popularity was of no consequence to me. I was getting aggravated at having to slip records I liked into my set sporadically between popular radio ear garbage. Finally, in 1996 I realized that the purists and followers of my style would be best served if I represented myself, so that is exactly what I did. I founded an independent production company and record label in Charlotte, NC called Sound Boy Records (later modified to "Soundboy") along with an insider magazine. I was 24 years old. I was unmarried, unattached and otherwise uninhibited.

Through editing the magazine and managing the label I realized that I was actually fulfilling an unspoken, unconscious lifelong ambition. My purpose was becoming apparent to me. Everything I learned was now being combined. But there was something missing. After four years I felt a certain passive aggression in promoting the music of other artists. I felt the need to create and perform again, but I did not have the patience or desire to be a full time professional musician. I hosted an open mic comedy show and I wrote for some of the comics. But I didn't want to tour or trade sixes as a comic either. The more I second guessed myself, the more I slipped into darkness. The only other thing I had ever been into besides music and writing was film. And just like that...I understood completely. I had written dozens of stories in High School and College. They all came back to me at once. I realized that they were actually scripts and screenplays. I held in my hands the final piece of the puzzle. This was the remainder of my purpose. I knew what I had to do to make it work, but I wanted to wait. I would not let myself (or rather my "self" would not let me) jump in to the unknown straight away.

For two years, I delayed my expansion into film while I learned about the film industry. I worked on film crews and attended film schools and boot camps. I paid my dues and patiently learned the art of light. I now understood that the various elements of my purpose were re-combining to carve out a cinematic style based on my musical and literary heritage. I made my first short film when I was 30 years old. It was shot on Hi-8 and transferred to 16MM. It consisted mainly of candid footage of comedy sketches being written, late night carousing at bars and behind-the-scenes concert footage. It could never have been a commercial success, but my crew and I loved it. Eventually I began to shoot music videos, which I regarded as short films set to music. The entire experience felt like home. I did not know how empty my soul was until it was filled. I had what artists called divine inspiration. I suddenly realized I could pool my collected resources and make them work for me.

I felt free. This was freedom as I understood it. I was promoting independent art outside the system while working on studio projects (and making my bones) within the system. It was everything I wanted it to be, but unfortunately it came to an abrupt end. The late 90's marked the beginning of the end for small production companies. The money that had previously gone into everyday production was now being paid to A-List actors. Studios no longer subcontracted to local companies. The 2nd age of the Hollywood blockbuster had begun. Companies like mine were still important to independent and art-house films, so I turned my attention exclusively to that. In some ways, we are still fighting a type of trench warfare against the major studios. We are trying to prevent the futility of independent artistry outside the mainstream. I realized that there is always price to pay for being a revolutionary. I could bring myself to abandon the ideals that brought me to that point. If I do not constantly do everything I can to push the envelope and continually seek the "gnosis" for myself and for those I have influenced or may influence in the future, then I can already claim to have failed. It is my purpose to always push forward as did my heroes and the true pioneers who have passed away. Through various mediums of artistic creation, I have come to personify my way of being and my ultimate nature. "Soundboy" is my alter-ego, as well as a reflection of my "self". Judging me by the vibe at yard parties and the records I play on my podcast is no different than judging me on my style of writing and making motion pictures. Everything is relative. "Times" change, but my standard will remain. My true identity will never abandon me. It is my heartbeat. It is a part of the way I speak and have always spoken. It is a part of my observations and social commentary. It is a part of my behavior and it is how I relate to others. It is my destiny to be exactly who I am. No more, no less. We must love who we are right now, just as we are – in order to strive for something higher. Every stone structure begins with the placement of one stone.

My goal is to contribute knowledge rather than withhold it; to cooperate instead of compete, so that my work can be combined with similar material to form the foundation of a new community and a better human society. Now more than ever I am learning to place value on the gnosis. Not to have or to own, but to share. Not to use as a weapon or shield but as a building block and stepping stone. After all these years as a writer, I finally understand how to interlace credit and credibility. I have a responsibility to research and share the gnosis and document my interpretation and understanding of its meaning and impact. In order to do this I must stand alone, at least in an artistic sense. I never asked anyone to fight my battles for me, or feel sorry for me. Things will shake out the way they shake out. I'm sailing on. When I see opportunities to demonstrate my relationship to the gnosis in an audible, visual and literary sense, I do what I can to live up to my human potential and fulfill my purpose. Regardless of circumstances we can always make an effort to "rise up"; mentally, physically, spiritually and emotionally. That's how life works.

If you want to become the idealistic version of yourself, continual introspection will lead to a realization of your ultimate nature, which is who you are right here and now. I am not afraid to voice my opinion or search for what I believe to be true, because from my perspective there are no consequences that outweigh the benefits of truth. I never set out to become some kind of Guru. My goal is to set an example of how things can get done – when you do it your way. Begin by making a distinction, finish by making a difference. Represent your destination to reflect your journey. If everything happens for a reason, we are all part of a universal machine in perpetual motion. It's ultimately your decision to make. Your reactions to the life you chose to live determine the ease or difficulty of your journey. You can either choose to go with the universe or choose to go against it. Either way, you are exactly where the universe wants you to be.

Chapter V

People who are racists enjoy being racists. They enjoy it the same way people who like horror movies enjoy being frightened, or people who like extreme sports enjoy the adrenaline rush. All of these personality types receive a sensation from a biochemical reaction caused by fear. The difference is, those who intentionally become frightened or overstimulated in a suspenseful manner do not generally translate their fear impulses into a social context; whereas those who exclude and restrict people based on race/ethnicity, age, gender, disability, sexuality, nationality or religion actually *require* those nervous system impulses and chemical reactions to function normally in society. They are emotionally no different than an alcoholic or drug addict. They are addicted to how they feel while being who they are. Is it possible for racists to transform themselves? Sure, if they wanted to, the same way a junkie or alcoholic becomes clean and sober. The problem is, they typically don't want to, unless acted upon or influenced by an external force or a genuine catharsis. Even if someone does experience a miraculous life-changing event which inspires them to drop their preconceived notions of race and culture, they are usually just trading one bigoted ideology for another. Would you rather have a racist neighbor who avoids you, or a bible-thumping two-faced neighbor who is all in your sauce constantly yakking about things they don't really understand? The moral is, when someone's a racist prick, even if they cease to be a racist, they would still be a prick – possibly to an even greater extent. During the late 70's in the midst of an unsuccessful attempt to combat the gathering unseen forces of a neo-conservative fascist plutocracy, a few liberal members of congress had the genius idea of appointing scientists – rather than sociologists or psychologists to study drug abuse and chemical dependency. Those scientists discovered something really interesting. They found that no substance – natural or synthetic, is in-and-of itself addictive.

The individual's biochemical reactions create the addiction, not the actual substance. In other words, drug addicts are psychologically addicted to the sensation of reaction, not the substance itself; which has equally as much to do with an individual's personality, environment and biochemistry. This is why some people can periodically ingest "controlled" substances and not become addicted. In my youth I smoked cannabis on a few occasions, but I never got anywhere near the high that some of my friends raved about. I used it to manage pain. I have been in constant pain for most of my adult life. I have an arthritic condition in which knots form in the tendons all over my body. Over time, I developed a high pain/tolerance threshold. My body can accommodate large quantities of painkilling opiate derivatives and other natural analgesics. I never set out to get "high". However, if that is your thing, be my guest. Plus, I don't consider natural substances "drugs". In my eyes, drugs are synthetic compounds made from petrochemicals and they do more harm than good. The intended purpose of natural psychedelic substances was to allow humans to commune with all beings on all planes of existence, not to escape reality. I have always enjoyed a refreshing beverage; a good lager, a Sonoma Valley Zen or bourbon Lime Rickey (and her sexy Cuban cousin, Mojito); originally as a causeway through inhibition then later to pacify my feelings of ubiquity and restlessness in regards to constantly doing whatever I wanted. It may be a liability, but it was never a problem. It never caused sensations to which I became physically or psychologically addicted. Although there were similar findings in people who were addicted to shopping, television, authority, gambling, sympathy, affection, food and sex, they were completely disregarded by the puppet Reagan regime; as they would have reduced the corporate profits earned in the state-sanctioned drug trade (legal and illegal). It would have also diminished the ranks of competitive, materialistic zombie-robots in the workforce. As a rule, corporations tend to prefer sick, dying consumers to productive human beings.

It's another example of reality vs. perception. You're either inside looking out or outside looking in – until you realize there is no outside or inside. Most people who commit suicide are not doing so because they *want* to die; they're doing it to take the pain away. That's reality from their perspective. We are conditioned, by the systems of control to automatically fear and reject reality, in much the same way we reject truth. The "reality television show" is a complete contradiction in terms. It is a false reality packaged and presented to those who refuse to face their own reality. As a result, throughout life people become more and more divergent and dissociative; they live vicariously through other people and sometimes even develop personality disorders in order to avoid their reality.

To understand this, try to understand the difference between a delusion and a hallucination. A delusion is often nothing more than a misinterpretation of an object that is physically real. For example, seeing the image of the Mona Lisa in a clump of trees or finding a goat that looks like John the Baptist is a delusion. However, riding in a paddleboat with John the Baptist is a hallucination. I admit that I have divergent personalities. I use what is called "artistic license" as a writer. These personas are fictional characters and I understand that they are not real. Their existence prevents me from strangling people. This is a common personality trait for creative people. I think it's useful for creative types to be at least slightly delusional, because the super-saturation of propagandist media makes everyone else at least slightly neurotic. Our overall perception of what we believe to be reality is a key to understanding our divine human origin and how self awareness has been replaced by religious dogma. Angels, for example are typically thought of as radiant feminine beings who are wise and gentle in appearance. However, according to the Bible, the Torah, the Tanahk, the Talmud and the Koran; angels are either masculine or genderless, more correctly referred to as "sons of Elohim"; superhuman entities who exist in multiple, simultaneous states of being, on multiple planes of existence.

They are sometimes anthropomorphic (animals or other beings with human characteristics) and often represented planets, stars or signs of the zodiac. It's interesting how easily Judaeo-Christian beliefs can be traced back to the worship of EL, the Phoenician-Canaanite god also known as Saturn. All the archangel's names also end with the suffix "EL"; Michael, Gabriel, Ariel, Azazel, Samael, etc. translated as "of or from God". These are the collective beings referred to by the authors of Genesis; *"let us make Man in our image after our likeness"*. In fact, during that era the most common words used in reference to God were plural; including Elohim (Gods), and Adonai (my Lords). In psalms these beings are referred to as the "congregation of the mighty" or "heavenly council". This plural usage is not a "royal plural" as some scholars would contend, as this phrase was an example of how people referred to God, not how God referred to himself. The 1st, 2nd and 3rd person grammatical context combination is very specific in Greek, Phoenician and Aramaic. When God did refer to itself, it would say "I am the Lord God", meaning lord-of-the-gods; or "I am the Lord *thy* God" meaning I am *your* God, but not necessarily the God of that guy over there who has fun with animals in a way you probably shouldn't. That guy's God is bananas. I wouldn't really mess with him if I were y'all. In any event, the belief in an existence of Angels most likely evolved from ancient civilizations perception of polytheism, despite how they are now perceived by modernity. In common usage, reality means "everything that exists" as opposed to that which is imagined. Reality includes both being and nothingness. However existence is apparently *restricted* to being. There are three levels in the conception of reality; truth, fact, and axiom (I.e. pseudo-subjectivity, proven occurrence and physical evidence). Perception is basically the process of acquiring and interpreting sensory information. We are able study human perception in both the biological sense as well as psychologically in the abstract via philosophy of the mind.

The resulting "thought experiments" are crucial to quantum physics and are sometimes put into practical use as "aesthetic realism". As an example, I remember a discussion I had with several friends at a dinner party several years ago, about a film directed by a friend on the topic of skin color and complexion in people of color. Although it became a heated discussion, it ended in comedic fashion thanks only to the dry satire which I have come to embrace. All in present company were either partially or entirely Afro-American or otherwise "of color". As the evening progressed someone had the bright idea to make a sly remark that because of our light complexion, I – and my lighter-skinned friends, would have been much better off during the time of slavery than those of a darker complexion. I immediately considered the statement a sign of severe insecurity. It had no bearing on modern society from my point of view. Making rhetorical arguments as hypothesis is usually irrelevant, much like those history channel shows about re-fighting ancient battles with modern weapons. This was pure speculation based mostly on assumption and only slightly interesting within a narrow context. If such a statement sparks a logical debate in relation modern society, that's fine with me. Otherwise it's pointless. I believe the statement was simply a device to make myself and certain others guilty and/or self-conscious about our skin color, which is something we cannot change. Rhetorical rationale seems offensive to me in this sense. It's a defense mechanism. There is no such thing as light or dark-skinned "guilt" as far as I am concerned; and I would never interpret history based on self-reflection. When physical slavery ended in the US, (and wage-debt slavery began) the social and economic system in which slaves were recognized had ended as well. I do however agree that there is scientific evidence that people are more or less "drawn" to others who are similar in appearance and/or cultural values. Some refer to this as the "self-reference criterion" and it has been recently co-opted by marketing firms for use in subliminal advertising.

The premise is that people unconsciously gravitate toward the similarities in others rather than differences. If that is the case, so be it. But it has nothing to do with my conscious behavior. I don't judge anyone based solely on skin color. Any problem you have with someone else's natural appearance is your problem entirely. Not to mention in some cases within slave society, lighter-skinned slaves were actually given *less* preferential treatment by planter-class whites; as they were seen as a constant reminder of a genetic link between master and slave; which also varied depending on geographical location and slave-owning culture. This fact alone basically questions the entire paradigm, but learned animosity is difficult to let go. So, I began to formulate yet another divergent persona to help illustrate my point. I began to tell my friends the story of my past alter-ego. His name is *Ole' Mister Skippy*, although there are a few permutations of his name; *Ole' Skippy*, *Skippin' Jim* etc. He lives in North Carolina during the mid-nineteenth century. He is a slave. He resides in a big house with the master and his family on a plantation. He is light complexioned. He lives in the attic, rather than the cellar, because he likes it hot. He wears an old, ill-fitting suit but keeps it fairly clean. He eats pretty well, but he doesn't eat very much.

On one particular occasion as he was teaching himself a dance routine, he was approached by some of his fellow slaves; "field-hands" who were darker skinned than he. "What cha' say, fellas". Skippy remarked. They suddenly began to jeer him and call him names like "house nigga" and "swell". "Oh, y'all are just calling me that because I live in the house". He replied. They told him that was exactly why they were calling him that. "Okay then" said Skippy. "Let me ask you this…what do you want? I'm trying to learn this here dance routine I made up just now". They told him he had an easy life in the house while they toil out in the field. "Well" he replied, "Y'all get nights off, and all Christmas-week. I work every goat-pissing day, all day long. [He begins to hum melodically] I feed the chickens and I chop wood too."

"Plus, I have to go out every Christmas Eve and chop down a big stupid-ass tree. Then drag it all the way back to the house!" Skippy became more agitated as their verbal abuse intensified. They told him that he was not one of them. They told him he wasn't black. Skippy got sore at that remark. "Y'all got some nerve! Especially after y'all told mosh Philip I stole some peaches last week. Them was pomegranates, asshole! Yet, I took a peach whooping for it". They said he was nothing more than the master's dog. "Well, no" he replied. "I'm probably more like a cat". The field-hands let him know that when the day of reckoning came, he would be on the wrong side. "Was that a question?" Skippy asked. They said they just wanted him to know. "Thank you", said Skippy, sarcastically. "Although, I don't know why you're bringing it up now, I'm 37 years old. Also…I know a few a' y'all got the same Pappy as me!! And…furthermore…in addition to that…I know one a' y'all stole my banjo!" As the field-hands laughed, Old Skippy became even more enraged. He knew that one of the slaves who were currently breaking his balls about being light-skinned had also previously stolen his banjo, but he couldn't prove it. So he decided to let it go. But it was eating him up inside. He didn't actually know how to play it, but that wasn't the point. He primarily used it to smash various rodents and marsupials over the head. Without it, he and other residents of the attic were now virtually helpless against raccoon, bat and possum attacks. Skippy eventually calmed himself enough to speak rationally. "I'm slightly better off in the house…but I'm still a slave, same as you...so I don't appreciate your face right now". As the field-hands walked away one of them said with a glib, sardonic smile to keep on dancing. "Thank you. I will, jerk!" he replied. "Hit it Richard!" Skippy said, and resumed his dance routine as his roommate Richard pounded on a bucket. But it was getting late, and he knew he had to help prepare the Masters' teenage daughters for bed. Typically, he would help prepare the shit out of them, on an average of 2-3 nights a week. But he was getting a little older now.

He had to save his strength for chopping wood, splitting raccoon wigs, etc. One night after "tucking in" two of the masters' daughters, he had a catharsis. He realized the field-hands had a point. He knew he could pick tobacco better than Medium Pete, who was darker than he, yet he was not allowed to do so. He also knew he could cook better than Extra-Large Amos, who was even lighter-skinned - and had a nicer bunk in the attic. He couldn't understand why they were being judged by complexion – or sub-divided, as they were all slaves regardless. And he wondered why he didn't likewise have a biblical name and size-descriptive epithet. The heated discussion with the field-hands made him realize how pointless his life really was. He just couldn't see it at the time, because he was upset about the banjo. After a few minutes of contemplation, he realized that the entire concept of slavery was morally wrong. It was not part of a "natural order". This infuriated him; but not enough to get out of bed just yet. The first one out of bed had to feed the chickens. His anger festered as he lay there a while with mixed feelings of guilt and remorse. He made a decision that from this moment on - as in first thing in the morning, he would dedicate his life to destroying the system of slavery from the inside. He would no longer be a "house nigga"; He would be a saboteur…a commando…a guerrilla warrior. It was subtle at first; super tangy oatmeal, beehives that appeared out of nowhere, loose steps on the front porch, chair legs sawed halfway through and piles of dog-shit without the immediate presence of a dog. After a while, he became more adept and aggressive; crop burning, realistic looking scarecrows in place of runaway slaves, rum bottles filled with water, undisclosed sources of meat, thus and so. He gradually began to realize his purpose in life. He regretted all the years he had spent obeying this asshole. He realized the master's entire existence depended solely on the obedience of the slave. He felt more energetic than ever before. From then on, he would not only "tuck in" the young Misses of the house but also their visiting female cousins.

In fact, he eventually spent more time "tucking in" plantation skanks than setting various booby traps. He felt that he needed to prioritize. Sabotage is hard work. It was a good idea to unwind a bit from time to time. One morning his so-called master called out for him in a panic. "Skippy!! Come Hyah, bwah!!" Skippy ambled over to his master who was greatly agitated. It appeared that he was stuck to his rocking chair. He told mister Skippy that he thought someone had poured glue onto the chair and asked him if he knew anything about it. "No Sir", Skippy replied. "All I know about it is what I'm being told right now." His master was now greatly annoyed. He asked Skippy how in the world that could have happened. Mister Skippy told him that he had no idea, then suggested that someone may have shellacked the chair as a surprise and forgot to tell him about it. His master then commanded Skippy to help him get out of the chair, as the hair on his ass was beginning to stick to the inside of his pant-leg. Mister Skippy paused for a moment in contemplation. "Look here, boss", said Skippy, "You stick around (pun), and I'll run and get help! Well...maybe not run...but I'll be back directly, I reckon...or something like that". But Skippy did not run and get help. He made a sandwich and took a nap. His master eventually had to duck-walk into the house with the chair stuck to his ass and cut his pants off with a pocket knife. Skippy took a really bad whipping for that. But as he saw it, all slaves take a whipping at some point, sooner or later. That's why it's best to live free, or die. A few years later the Civil War began, and his plantation terrorism intensified. More random chair gluing, marbles on the floor at the top of the staircase, holes dug in the floor covered by rugs, works of art stolen and replaced with his own sketches and watercolors, children born with mysteriously nappy hair, accurate land surveys and topographical maps for invading Union Armies, etc. A Union Captain once asked Skippy why one map had holes poked in it. "The holes represent holes", said Skippy. When the war was finally over, so was the southern way of life.

Ironically, this now put Skippy at a great disadvantage. Mister Skippy was not a farmer or a hunter or a fisherman. He knew how to read and write, but he didn't have the patience to be a teacher. Plus his lofty writing style rubbed folk the wrong way. He had no way to earn a living. He could not sustain himself in a hostile environment in which all human rights were denied to those who had previously been slaves. He had very little recourse, so he reluctantly decided to go north. He settled in Milwaukee and applied all of his moonshining & bootlegging knowledge to creating high quality, low-end pilsner. Years later, before he died, he realized that even though he became a nuisance, he could never change the cultural mentality that was responsible for the "institution" of slavery. Sure, he could urinate in everyone's oatmeal, but when he forgot to set some aside for himself, he felt a sort of righteously indignant starvation. Sure, he could stick beehives under the sofa, but he couldn't always run away fast enough without getting stung a few times. The point is, what he did may have made life more difficult for those who were in turn making life difficult for others, but in the long run, it did not have as much impact as slaves who refused to work or ran away. It did not have the impact of former slaves returning to fight for what they believed was their freedom. It did not have the impact of slaves creating a culture from scratch and carving out a life for themselves under the worse possible conditions. Of course the legend of Ole' Mister Skippy is fictional, but a part of him that exists in some of us today, mostly me. I understand now as Ol' Skippy did back then, that it is impossible to change a system while remaining as a part of that system. It is only possible to destroy it. This light and dark skin dichotomy only has meaning to the brothers and sisters who are bound by the limits of their neurosis or insecurity. Some of us may also identify with this paradigm to keep from asking deeper questions. But I wont entertain preconceived notions of how I am supposed to behave when confronted with a pointless, subjective hypothetical. Life is too short to wonder what it would be like as someone else.

You have to be who you are, even if you aren't sure who that is. I know who I am now. I know my divergence is in many ways a coping mechanism. It prevents me from choking people out on a regular basis. I have always been attracted to having and alter ego. My first divergent personalities appeared when I was a child. I had various personas that I would step into if necessary. I never actually pretended to be another person; I just allowed my alter egos to take over my psyche when needed. They weren't really "imaginary" friends, because they didn't exist as a separate being outside my mind. I'm sure they would have fought my battles more often, but sometimes I just couldn't get into character fast enough. As a young child I frequently got into scrapes with groups of other kids, who were usually bigger and stronger than I was. I never seemed to have a problem with anyone "mano e mano", only when dudes formed cliques and got fresh with their mouth a little. I started grade school early at age 4 but I found a group of friends who were about a year older and we became a pretty tight crew for the next 15 years or so. But when they were not around, I got hassled continually. My smart mouth had something to do with it, never knowing when or how to back down.

I understand that boys are going to fight, in school and elsewhere. That's just the way it is. But I was regularly singled out, because I stood out. I was unapologetically precocious. Adults generally liked me, but I didn't get along well with most other kids. After a few years, I decided to finally bring a proverbial gun to the knife-fight, so to speak. I began to incorporate the help of gawky, awkward girls in my class who had a crush on me. I would describe to them how the bullies had attacked me and how I felt powerless to do anything about it. This plan worked better than I ever could have imagined. Oh, how grand it was to see a 5-foot, 125 pound grade school girl beating the absolute piss out of some annoying, snaggletooth hayseed who was pushing me around. It was as if God was kneeling down from heaven to kiss me gently on the forehead.

Some kids occasionally had a go at me because I supposedly let a girl do my "fighting". But I just shrugged it off. No one ever said pimpin' was easy. I felt like I was in *Harem Scarem* except I had a 4-foot tall egg-shaped 3rd grade she-devil instead of Mary Ann Mobley. It is much to my benefit that I have never really embraced either pride or embarrassment. This is yet another (and most prevalent) one of my character contradictions; being privately self-conscious yet having almost no regard for anyone's opinion of me. I admit that it is confusing. It's a part of the negative vs. positive self-consciousness war that I wage against myself continuously. As a teenager, I mistakenly saw the contradictions in my character as irreparable. Instead of trying to sort it out, I intentionally created additional conflict to compensate. It's like when kids join a gang for protection…from that very gang.

This logic seems reasonable from a teen's point of view, because teenagers' brains are not fully developed, regardless of their intelligence level. They all need some form of consistent, positive human interaction. On several occasions as a teen I found myself in situations that were entirely my fault and could have easily been avoided. I went beyond the theoretical hedge, as it were. My spiritual friends know this as karma. My parents referred to it simply as the "hedge theory" in reference to the biblical book of Job. *"Have you not put a hedge around him and his household and everything he has? You have blessed the work of his hands," Job 1:10.* The hedge is a metaphor for Gods' hands surrounding him, acting as a hedge against evil. Theoretically, inside the hedge I was doing God's will (whatever that is) but outside the hedge I drew his contempt and was in mortal danger. Except Job never stepped outside the hedge. God just removed it to prove a point. When I was a kid, I thought to myself "that was kind of a dick move. "Super not cool, God. I want my 5 dollars back." But I get it now. The bible is a compilation of human and superhuman composite characters and contextual metaphors written in code. It is literature based on allegorical myth.

If you can't understand that, you will never really understand the bible. I lose patience with fundamentalists who interpret the bible 100% literally because they don't want to understand those literary concepts. They will defend a completely literal interpretation - except when it doesn't support the official narrative. So the point is, it doesn't matter if God removes the hedge from around you (for whatever reason) or if you intentionally go beyond it, because the result is the same. It doesn't necessarily mean that God is a jerk – or that you were doing something you weren't supposed to do. It essentially adds up to "shit happens; big-up, and move on", i.e. *"The Lord giveth, and the Lord taketh away; Blessed be the name of the Lord". Job 1:21.* As an adult, this concept should be fairly easy to grasp, but for the majority of folk nowadays it somehow isn't. However, children have difficulty with metaphors, so I tried my best to stay inside the metaphoric hedge as if it were an actual hedge. I was not always successful. I was fortunate that the understated yet overdeveloped girls who protected me did not lose their motivation to do so because of my new-found arrogance. But in my defense, I played my part, with valentine's treats, candy and fruit in addition to letting them hold my hand which I can only imagine was a great thrill for them [arrogance]. (Women of all ages require attention. If you are with a special lady and you don't pay attention to her, believe me, someone else will.) Ultimately, I took my pre-pubescent harem for granted, and when they were not around I paid the price. I also unintentionally created friction among them, igniting playground cat-fights which began with the familiar war cry "Uh-Uh, girl! He's my Man!" followed by a lot of slapping and shoving and flying off of coke-bottle glasses, beaded jewelry and plastic hair barrettes. It was awful and beautiful at the same time. Like the way Brother Bonaparte described Moscow in flames. Their fighting was not a welcome site, but they would never really hurt each other. It was more of a wild kingdom/new wilderness style display of aggression to ward off their rivals.

There were never any lasting hard feelings and schoolyard fights of that nature were quickly forgotten. I accepted the necessity of fighting. As I grew bigger and stronger, I realized a sort of natural coordination. I learned how to fight and how not to fight. By my early teens, most physical confrontations were avoided. But I carried a lot of bitterness in general. I understand now that I had been singled out for *what* I was, not *who* I was. My appearance was unique, the way I spoke unusual and the stories I wrote were difficult to read. So, I routinely tried to keep a low profile. I eventually embraced a laid-back style and calm demeanor, which I guess is unusual for an adolescent. But maybe that was part of the reason I didn't fit in. I suppose by not acting like a typical grade school maniac I seemed threatening somehow.

At the time, I would rather have been bullied or picked-on straight up about regular kid-stuff instead of being constantly alienated for my creativity. I now understand that bullies are made, they're not born. They are just misguided pricks with assholes for parents. Their home life causes them to turn "you" problems into "us" problems. All adolescents are already insecure to some degree. Getting browbeaten daily by some twonk doesn't help. So I am unsure as to whether I became a teenage rude boy by choice or by consequence. I ditched school as much as I could (hence the moniker "Skip"). I felt that I wasn't learning anything of value, so why bother. I saw myself on the edge of normality, unwilling to submit to the system. Normal is boring. Average is dull. I tried to embrace diversity no matter where I was or what I was doing. Diversity is one of the few redeeming characteristics our society has. We live in a world where most people feel that they have to look and act a certain way at all times based on a set criteria. We are a selfish and self-centered society in the most selfish place on earth. I currently live in the very non-indigenous Southeastern US. I understand that some people want to keep their regional identity when they move here, but that's not enough reason to run down the place in which you currently reside.

Everyone has preferences. Try not to go around criticizing an area based on your subjective validation or other such cognitive bias. Many of the giants in Be-Bop were born in North & South Carolina. Jazz originated in New Orleans and revolutionized the world of entertainment. The Delta blues men who traveled to Texas to make records became heroes of later generations. Rock and Roll would have never existed if not for the Southern rhythm and blues giants that crafted their art despite horrific social conditions and almost complete lack of compensation. Some people of color actually stayed here in the South under the most horrible conditions, while others went North in search of employment and security. Neither decision was right or wrong. It was simply a choice based on the experience of the individual and their immediate family in relation to their environment. When my family moved south in the Mid 70's, I experienced for the first time divisions within my own culture. People drew attention to how fair-skinned I and my sisters were and related it to how they thought we should behave, although they knew nothing about us whatsoever. Prior to moving South, we lived in New England. That type of petty indignation didn't really exist in our community. During that era, you were either white...or you weren't. Period. It didn't matter how light-skinned you were, if you were a Negro, that was that. We were all in the same boat, so to speak – no pun intended. Nowadays I generally encourage people to express their opinions on culture, rather than keeping it bottled up and putting a strain on relationships. We can't change the past or hold someone directly accountable for acts in which they took no part. However, we can acknowledge white privilege and colonial imperialist culture and work toward destroying both. Traditionally it's known as "sins of the father", a real concept that has little to do with common perception. I don't believe in the idea of "sin", but I do understand natural law. Unfortunately, some people must reap that which their forefather hath sewn. This type of "sin" is basically planting the seeds of karmic justice, which will always prevail.

I am still unsure about justice administered by the universe as a "deserved" punishment or reward, because life is not about what we deserve. Although I identify culturally with the American Negro, I never really felt as if I was completely a part of any one specific ethnic group. I'm a man. I'm human. I'm fighting desperately to keep from having personage (incorporation). Someday, ethnicity will be merely a conversational topic instead of a tool of pre-judgment or a rough measure of character. But until then, most people will see and notice it first. When I was a child, I lived within two conflicting versions of ethnic and cultural reality. Half of my family lived in the South; the other half was divided between the Northeast and the West. At the start of the Puppet Reagan era, our family was equal to most others in our neighborhood. We lived in a historically black, rural working-middle class area. No one in the neighborhood was considered very wealthy or very poor. We retained some sense of community. The ignorance of so-called wealth was not a hindrance to wellbeing.

However, the lack of priority given to social status was made up for by judgment of physical appearance. When we moved south for the first time, I was amazed how much value and emphasis was put on complexion and various non-ethnic features and characteristics in the black community. I had never even thought of considering someone's complexion as a basis for any kind of assessment. In the Northeast we were seen as light-skinned Negroes, but Negroes nonetheless. We were also a product of our time as well as environment. Not very many Negroes or Native Americans in the 70's would (or could legally) acknowledge their shared lineage. The civil rights era had given way to a new constructionist "nationalism" in the US. Gone were the days of Harry Belafonte's vision of racial harmony in a homogenized society. It was replaced by a commercially driven need to identify with one particular culture and immediately judge others who do not. Although not socially acceptable, I do feel that certain forms of judgment are necessary. Judging is how we get through life intact.

Just be prepared to have others judge you in return. Judgment differs from prejudgment as judging should include some element of instinct and experience. Prejudice is a mental state, made of preconceived notions. Acting on said prejudice is how discrimination is born. If my childhood experience occurred right now, (post Cosby show) my family would not even seem unique. By the 90's, most people mistook my family's Native American features for Middle-Eastern, which created more unnecessary discussion. My immediate family is of color. My father is light-skinned. My mother was light brown skinned. My sisters and I, who are somewhere in-between, were often looked down on by our peers outside our extended family. We were in some degree ostracized by many dark-skinned black kids and patronized by most white kids (as it seemed that we made them uncomfortable) and there were not enough other minorities around to balance the equation. Ironically, the few "biracial" kids whom we did know actually identified with their Caucasian parent, completely ignoring their nappy hair and olive skin as if it were a fluke.

At the same time, I and my light-skinned friends who had Native ancestry were conditioned to ignore it, as if it were inconsequential. Although we had several even lighter-skinned cousins, their hair was slightly nappier and their lips were fuller, so no one ever questioned their "Negritude". For the record, ethnic hair does not have to be coarse in order to be nappy. I have fine baby-style hair, but it is nappy like a goat's ass. (That's probably why I have only ever had 3 distinct hairstyles in my entire life; a curly afro, an MLK/Rudeboy fade and the "Guigro" [*Guido/Negro*] wavy low-skin fade 20's-era playboy Haile Selassie/Max Baer combo which I often sport nowadays.) As children, not being able to fully relate to our peers was just annoying at first, but later it became a psychological strain. No one ever talked about it because no one ever wanted to acknowledge that it was actually happening. Had it not been for the Spike Lee film *School Daze* in 1986, it may have taken decades for anyone to acknowledge it.

That film was a fictionalized account of a real social issue. Although it was somewhat over-dramatized, it had a basis in truth, as does most cultural art and almost all cultural stereotypes. Our parents were very liberal in the 70's, borderline radical in fact. They did not teach us to behave defensively in our own community, as any threats would most likely be external. They taught us instead to understand the reasons behind other people's behavior toward us. Theoretically, everyone should instill that type of virtue in their children. But from a practical point of view, it just couldn't work. Understanding someone's motives for spite and aggression is meaningless to a child. Children need to understand that they are safe, secure and protected. We were imbued with such a "black-first" mentality, that we were more easily taken advantage of by our classmates of color than by anyone outside of the community. My parents, being brought up during the segregation era retained a sense of community that was much stronger than ours, because it was out of necessity. But by the early 80's all bets were off. The worm had turned. The Puppet-Reagan Neocon era had begun and the 70's Black Nationalist renaissance came to an end. My parents separated amicably and I split my time between them, trying not to become bitter. I was able to curb my hard feelings and channel my frustration into creativity due to my parents' encouragement. I discovered art, music and film; and I began to write more proficiently. Living in the Northeast, in mostly white urban (pre-redlined) neighborhoods, was a stark contrast to living in the South, where it seemed we participated in a voluntary segregation. While living up North I had a welcomed sense of security, but I completely lacked any camaraderie or true fellowship with kids my age. I didn't realize it at the time, but the two living conditions set in juxtaposition were shaping my personality. My early experience with this cultural climate shift would later re-combine with similar experiences to strengthen my character. I was building myself; out of diverse bricks using mortar mixed with the sands of time.

However, this duality of culture made me somewhat jaded to simplistic country-style values, which I began to resent. I feel that the apathy I displayed in my teens was a direct result of the lack of continuity and ethnic diversity, from north to south. I could not feel strongly about social issues, so I would therefore not feel strongly about anything. I didn't know if my behavior was right or wrong, but I know it *felt* right. Enigmatic, esoteric, agnostic anarchy suited me. It still does. I always found it strange that so many people put such a great deal of faith in political systems and government. My struggle is only political by consequence, so I have very few political views. My philosophy is; take care of "self", take care of home, take care of family, take care of community - and the truth will be revealed as a matter of course. I refuse to accept systemic (corporate) definitions of the human condition. My ultimate reality is opposed to the majority perception. When I started my career, most people saw me as a grounded, focused, intelligent young man, who could go as far as he wanted within the system. That was the truth, but it wasn't the reality. In reality I had already removed myself from the system. Focus determines reality just as freedom determines consciousness. Time after time I created an illusion of someone considered to be the social definition of success, and time after time I intentionally held myself back from it. I had contempt for myself as a person, but I had complete admiration for myself as a human being. I was secretly ashamed of myself for taking part in discussions of my eventual mainstream success. The more people liked who I was, the more I hated the person I was becoming. But in that conflict I found a comforting humility. I decided to seek and embrace dual truth no matter how brutal the process. By understanding universal truth I could identify and straighten out the inequities that stood in the way of my self-awareness and self-awakening. On the flip-side however, I always tend to restrict or constrain my ultimate nature because it is the one thing I am wary of. I sometimes remove myself from myself - in order to protect myself.

Eventually, I learned to embrace my true character in order to form a new reality. As a young writer, I never pushed myself hard enough to meet deadlines and accomplish my goals within a reasonable amount of time; although I had no problem pushing myself to the edge for other things that I wanted. I often wanted things I didn't *need* but for some reason wanted to *have*. This mentality is the prevailing consensus in our societal system. Today I look back and laugh at the concepts of material possession, private property and conservatism. I understand now that knowledge of self is more important than any possession or ideology. I will never again be a slave to materialism. Those who can't (or refuse to) see beyond the material realm are part of a false paradigm. They are prisoners of a corporeal consciousness, confusing meaning with purpose. Meaning is empty without reason. Purpose is intrinsic, *not* incidental. Matter is not all that matters. The purpose of everything in existence is interconnected. All matter, including dark-matter and antimatter are a part of a universal plan of existence. Aristotle believed that all objects in existence have purpose; and their final purpose is to realize their eventual perfection. Ayn "the man" Rand ironically wrote "purpose must be one of the three ruling values of human life, the other two values being reason and self-esteem". When I was young, I believed that the concept of all things having a purpose (much like the concept of good and evil) was too simple to be true. But now I understand that truth is in fact simplicity; and even if we consciously attempt to reject our purpose, our destiny is still predetermined. So, how can we tell the difference between them? One must be the driving force for the other, but which one is which? As I began to question how the two concepts could co-exist without conflict, I immediately understood their relationship to each other and to everything else. Purpose is the perception, destiny is the reality. The two are positively symbiotic, or interdependent. Free will is an illusion of this symbiosis. Choice is a balance of conscious and unconscious, but is also predetermined.

Everything we appear to control is actually preordained. We have to start thinking on another level entirely. It begins with an understanding of how systemic our world has become. In 2007, I stated that the Corporation known as the United States would never have an African-American president; and technically, I am still correct. The current president of the corporation doesn't quite fit the legal criteria of Afro-American, in that as an "Anglo/American-Kenyan" he kind of skipped that step. However, he is legally and undoubtedly a Negro or Person of Color. Anyone born in the US who has a traceable black ancestor is legally "of color", (known as the one-drop rule) which intentionally creates a large cultural group. Adversely, in order to be considered legally Jewish, your *mother* has to be Jewish; regardless of the father's ethnicity, thereby intentionally creating a much smaller cultural group. The definition of Afro-American is having one or both parents with current valid US citizenship and being of African or Negro descent. Legally, I am an Afro-American. Both my parents are legally Afro-American, although they each have a parent who is part Native American. Having a Native American parent, grandparent, great grandparent (and in some states great, great grandparent) makes someone a Native American, but only *legally* if the tribe is "recognized". This rule was primarily adopted to prevent Negroes from "passing" as Natives and vice-versa. Now, I'm not trying to encourage weird annoying racists who actually think the US Corporation would appoint someone as president who didn't have a birth certificate. The oligarchs are not that dumb. I am just pointing out that if he and I were standing together and someone said "point out the Afro-American", you could only correctly point to me. By legal definition, according to my stock certificate (our birth certificates are legally considered stocks by the corporation) I'm a legal Afro-American subsidiary of the US corporation, even though some of my ancestors were Tri-Racial Isolates or "Melungeons" and were legally considered "free people of color" by the state of NC, instead of slaves.

Creating this legal distinction eventually backfired. Unlike the biracial Creoles and former slaves who purchased their freedom, the "Carolinian Algonquin Negroes" were very anti-establishment. The original goal was to create a "managing overseer" class, but ironically the state created a class of skilled laborers, artists and artisans who owned property and openly engaged in commerce. State lawmakers realized their error and recognized the multiethnic tribe as the Lumbee. Some of my other ancestors, who were descendant from Siouan tribes rather than Algonquin, were encouraged to hide their Native ethnicity as late as the mid-20th century, as Federally recognized tribes had limited citizenship. All my other ancestors can be traced back to just about every other source; African slaves, Scottish pirates, French immigrants and so on. No direct offense is intended toward Barack, as he is definitely a man of color. But the perception of him as an Afro-American is based on a false presumption - by the corporations own standards.

Realistically however, if you are "of color" and you are born within the corporation's borders, you get thrown onto a very large pile of "minorities", although in a few generations we will actually become the majority. The real irony of how most people feel about Barry O exists as a subliminal stimulus paradigm, almost in a paradoxical sense. The nutty white supremacists and right-wing apologists of color who hate the corporation's president share two very basic misunderstandings. First, if you would just shut up about him, you would realize that many people of color don't really care for him either. We just don't say anything publicly because you are <u>always</u> running him down and talking greasy. Secondly, it doesn't matter who is appointed as president because right and left wing politics - as flip sides of the same coin, are nothing more than a continuation of the same hypocrisy. There have only been two presidents thus far who have gone against the interests of the US corporation in favor of its "citizens". They were both murdered and all their policies were reversed. All other presidents are simply company men.

Chapter VI

When I am in public, during my leisure time, from October to April, I am generally dressed like a mid-1960's South London Mod. By that I mean, straight out of a Mick Antonioni film. It's a style I am most comfortable with. I can't always pull it off, however. It doesn't work if I'm too pudgy or have that *Boo-Yah Tribe* prison yard-style build. When I'm in great physical shape however, playing the role of the svelte yeoman, my vintage leather loafers, snug bell-bottoms and fitted poly-cotton wing-collar shirt screams "Oh yeah, this cat is hep! Deal with it. You seem like an anodyne prick in comparison. His life is continually interesting, and he has awesome conversations with remarkable people". But on the other hand, when I'm kind of fat, the exact same outfit screams, "Yeah, he's probably a confused homosexual, who is angry at his parents". The "hep" effect is lost with the addition of 30lbs.

Now, I'm not implying by any means that husky fellas should give up the "mod" look or lifestyle, but I am suggesting that everyone should wear clothes that fit their body type. If you're a lady and you're sporting a full-on beer-baby or if you're muffin toppin' out of control, you should probably wear garments that are loose and free-flowing. Although very few men in my neck of the woods emulate mod style, I still don't get a lot of unusual reactions as I follow my everyday routine, which is typically banal. Most people probably think I am Southern-European. That's fine with me. I like the fact that it doesn't seem odd that I am in a supermarket squeezing melons instead of on stage with the *Yardbirds.* But don't get me wrong, I don't over-do it. I don't stroll around town wearing a neckerchief like Fred from Scooby-Doo. I just hook up fly pant-shirt-shoe combos and slide around the city getting my game straight. I could theoretically start a trend, but I doubt it. Any future mainstream or pop culture trending by me is unlikely. I am happy being a one-man revolution. I don't see myself the way that most other people see me.

In the long run, that is for the best. My admirable self-denial is just a perception, it isn't the reality. I don't have contempt for myself nor do I have any feelings of self-reverence. I just feel that what I'm saying isn't what most people are hearing - and how I appear isn't what most people are seeing. This may be difficult to explain and understand because I have never really tried to explain it to anyone - and I never really expected anyone to understand it. I have always, and will forever, truly connect with only a very small group of people. This theory is also known as the "Six Percent" theory, in reference to the group of people who make up 6% of the world's population; who connect, relate and communicate with each other instinctively (some even say telepathically) regardless of their environment or location. I can't say for certain that this theory is valid, but I accept it nonetheless, based on my own feelings and observations. Most cynics and narrow minded pseudo-intellectuals label me a contrarian, because I seem to continually disagree with the other 94%.

I use garden-variety run of the mill folks as my socio-meter. If certain people seem to enjoy a movie, album or book, I usually know immediately that I will never enjoy it, under any circumstance. In fact, sometimes I will go out of my way to ask people - who are painfully ordinary and dull, about things they like, just so I will know to avoid them. I keep this arcane perspective to myself. It doesn't serve any purpose to pontificate about things that I like and don't like. I'm equally sure that I don't listen when other people do that. If someone expresses a mild like or dislike to me in conversation, I rarely ask them why; because I usually don't care. I can always make small talk, but I can never pretend to be interested in triviality just to placate someone. Small talk should stay small. I am also unusually empathetic for a deconstructionist. I always see the human beneath the person, which always makes the person look corrupted. Socially, we learn to expect certain behavioral patterns from people in particular cultures or environments, thus creating a paradigm for their behavioral patterns.

Most so-called celebrities for example, are typically famous because they either completely reject or embrace these patterns; and they always seem to either love or hate who they are. They seem to be both relatable and mysterious at the same time. That is probably why celebrity gossip television and internet are so popular. But celebrity is a false paradigm. The largest group of celebrities simply made a conscious decision to strip themselves of any system of values under the pretext of having principles and beliefs; but realistically for money, fame and notoriety, all the while convinced that they have maintained their integrity. The remaining celebrities are the standard, doing nothing more than mindlessly repeating or mimicking the larger group. The smaller group represents the majority of television "programming". Both groups have dedicated themselves to doing whatever the public wants them to do. They are all slaves to a pop-culture consensus and the media manipulators. In the 16th century these court jesters took orders from royalty. Today Hollywood magnates take orders from captains of industry.

The exact same rule generally applies to politics except politicians are required to constantly sound like droning idiots, reciting contrived and hypnotic phrases and useless socio-political nonsense. Business, political and religious ambition, much like celebrity, is tied to society's textbook definition of success. My disdain for which is the reason I refuse to define success in any terms other than individual resolution and goals as a human being. My critics claim that I refuse to define success because I somehow fear and revile it. This can't be true. To be completely honest, I don't really fear anything anymore. I don't care enough about success to fear it And I don't fear failure. No one should. Failure is key to the experimental process. Failure contains more positive than negative components. It is essential to growth and development. Failure is how we learn what not to do. Failure is how we eliminate that which does not function properly. Failure is how we identify liabilities. I have no interest in society's definition of failure; because society itself futile. It is a "completeness" of failure.

I also refuse to define and/or measure success or failure in terms of materialism or possession. Based on those criteria, it would be logical for all intelligent people to be wary of that which society defines as success rather than failure. There is a very simple reason for this – the shared element of corruption. Professional communicators or conversationalists always advise people never to get into arguments about Politics, Religion or Money, which not coincidentally are the same three combined systems of control that keep you running on your hamster wheel made of cyclical consumption and fear. The reason given for avoiding such topics is because it's supposedly impossible to ever win such arguments, so why bother. But the real reason for avoiding these topics is the 300lb gorilla staring you right in the face, which all three things have in common; corruption, which is a *built in* component of all three systems. None of them could function without it. If these things were represented as an engine, corruption would be a vital and irreplaceable part. There is no such thing as business ethics or religious freedom or financial stability – those are constructs used to mask how these machines actually function.

I find it amusing when evidence of corruption is suddenly "made public" by the media and everyone acts surprised and horrified. Try to understand that this is the only way these machines can function. Do you realize that the poorly constructed, unstable, lean-to wood shack known as capitalism and its fiat petro-dollar currency scam are held together by the nails of corruption? Try to realize that the Modern Roman and Saturn Imperial cult is statistically the largest theoretical pimp, slumlord and drug dealer that has ever existed? Have you ever noticed that political idealism is no different than political realism and is nothing more than glad-handing, greenmailing, blackmailing and cut-throat extortion? Why on earth would anyone ever be surprised to hear the truth about it? It would be more surprising if we never heard about it. It occurs continually. It has to. If there was no element of corruption in these systems, they would immediately collapse.

Take for example the phrase "organized crime". In the early 20th century, politicians and their supporting business interests were responsible for organizing it; for the purpose of distribution and consolidation in the international drug trade, labor manipulation and all forms of vice using the ethnic sense of family and community as a form of regimental control. If you feel that any of this data is inaccurate, you are encouraged to do your own research. Many reasonable and pragmatic people would disagree with the concept of built in systemic corruption, because they cannot imagine anything other than the official television and scholastic version of how these systems are designed to work. We have been taught to revere and obey these systems since birth. Not doing so draws attention to us as a dysfunctional person, rather than to the system itself as an entirely corrupted entity. Beneath the element of corruption, the combined systems are partially fueled by the premise that you can never obtain enough of anything, no matter how much you already have; wealth, power, fame the "grace of god" and so on. Money is something we are taught from day one that we could never possibly have enough of. If you have a million, you could have ten million. If you have ten million, you should go for a half billion and so on. The carrot and the stick is the same in every system of control; "you too can be rich someday!" or "give me money and I will make sure you get into heaven!" or "vote for me and I will make sure you live the way you want!" It's a fantasy. It's a false reality. It only exists because you accept it - and by your participation, you perpetuate it. Most people never even come close to making the kind of money they have been hypnotized into thinking they can earn in their lifetime. Yet market culture completely stigmatizes any lack of material possessions. We have been conditioned to equate materialism with success. To think any other way is regarded as mentally unsound. We perpetuate the hoax of materialism as a necessity because we have been drawn into the tornado of fear and consumption.

The social formula for a "successful" life becomes more and more hollow and materialistic. Good grades = a good school = a good job = a good home = a good family = a good career = good retirement = a good coffin = a good funeral = a good burial = a good obituary. Is that when the cradle-to-the-grave social mind control and manipulation finally ends? Does our complicity in this system make it impossible for the next generation to break the cycle? Is it even possible to live in the modern world as we know it without paying the price of servitude? The answer is yes. But the devil is literally in the details. The personality contrasts that combine to make some people so unusually selfless are the bi-product of a virtue known as sacrifice. Outside of parenthood, sacrifice is something most people never *want* to do, but eventually succumb to an overwhelming compulsion. But even then, some people never make real sacrifices, just the appearance thereof. It seems that guilt and remorse will never be stronger than lust and greed. Human beings have simply gone too far in the direction of personage. The concept of sacrifice is not continuously beaten into our heads like the concept of materialism. There are not many pop songs that feature a sense of community. There are no how-to books on feeding the poor or instructional videos on modifying your rate of consumption – because that would be contrary to how the system functions. However, there are several pop-culture deceptions designed to convince people that they are indeed making a sacrifice. Unfortunately, eating healthy, exercising, energy conservation, recycling, etc., are not real sacrifices, because we are supposed to be doing all that anyway. Charitable contributions, for example, especially do not qualify as sacrifice because in addition to being tax-deductible social hangouts they are also a complete scam. Most donation proceeds go toward administrative costs and employee salaries while they pretend to fund research. So-called "charities" are also sponsored by corporations that perpetuate conditions and diseases for which the charities were set up in the first place.

No one should ever expect credit for virtue. Introspection should serve more than a philosophic purpose; it should put our entire life into perspective and help us understand the trappings of materialism and selfishness. Sure I want that fly sweater I saw in the magazine, I'm a minimalist. I want what I want. But I know I don't need it. I know that cost could benefit elsewhere. It would be cool to have a high-tech watch, but that money could buy coats and shoes for children of a working-poor family. My wants never outweigh my needs. I know that possessions are just things. Most of it is useless and you can't take any of it with you. The "finer things in life" should relate only to your life and your experience, not your epicurean divergence Creating yourself as a great human being is important. It's not about what you are, but *who* you are. I am a part of a small minority who would rather face social ambiguity than avoid or ignore it. I do so not because I believe a consensus is important, but because I believe that it isn't. The aspects of my personality should tell you nothing about me, but to most people, it tells them all they need to know. Their perception is not reality, but even if it were, the reality is not complete. Incomplete realities are like ghosts in the machine. Excess is systemic. I reject it as a matter of course. As a minimalist I avoid the paradox. I don't appear to be what I really am, so according to society, either something is wrong with me - or something wrong with you. But neither answer is correct. There is no right or wrong. To avoid being a prisoner of society and a slave to the system, you must understand the concepts of sacrifice and excess. In my life thus far, I have already turned down more money than some people will ever earn. When I make that statement in a public setting, I sometimes receive legitimate threats of violence. People can't process that way of thinking. Historically, my family has been neither rich nor poor. We do alright for themselves. Any of us could have been wealthy, but we preferred having a soul. We fight and argue, as do most. But there is no "bad blood", and no hard feelings other than occasional cautionary avoidance.

Both sides of my family have traditionally thrived in contribution to the professions of masonry, clergy, psychology, social work and agriculture; and I rejected them all. I turned down all opportunities to follow in footsteps or take over family businesses. My parents were not always happy about that, but they always understood. I wanted to write. I wanted to create. I wanted to influence. I have been writing, taking pictures and recording since I was five years old. Even if I could go back in time and change my course of action, I would not. The model or paradigm that I have built of myself since I was a child is exactly what I see when I look at myself in the mirror. Ideally, it should be what others see when they look at me, but that may never be the case. Ironically, I am almost exactly who I thought I would be as a professional adult. At times I'm slightly fatter and not quite as genial as I thought I would be, but other than that, I am my idealistic version of manhood set forth by my adolescent mind. I feel that an important part of manhood is how I see myself and the kind of impression I make on those around me. I try to take things that must be done as a matter of course and combine them with things that interest me. This tends to produce an atmosphere of comfortability. I'm comfortable with myself so I can therefore be comfortable with others. But it isn't always about the essence or appearance of comfort. I am generally more comfortable in public dressed in evening attire, provided that my clothes fit me well and are functional. The curious career combination of writer and pirate radio disk jockey usually affords me the opportunity for peripheral leisure activities. I try to represent myself through patience and sensibility instead of constant compromise. Thus, I have avoided becoming overly stereotypical, at least from my point of view. I have some nice clothes that probably cost more than average, but I never purchased anything I couldn't afford and I do not possess clothing that I do not wear. My paramount object is not to make myself more attractive; it is to demonstrate my ability to dress and groom myself properly as a grown man in order to attract a suitable mate.

I'm not afraid to get dirty because I enjoy getting clean. I'm not opposed to wearing track sneakers but I am usually more comfortable in casual shoes. Everything in my environment has a purpose. It's a fairly simple concept and it has nothing to do with excess. Most people have a per-conceived model of themselves but very few will ever admit it. The point is, if you are an adult and you do what everyone else thinks you should do most of the time, you have already compromised your integrity. I'm not trying to justify my interest in developing a unique style of apparel, but I do feel comfortable talking about my interests because I live within my means and I don't harm anyone. But symbiosis is relative. If I earned half the income, I would have half the wardrobe. I place no real value on any of it. I wish I could find several lightweight, comfortable jumpsuits I could wear on a daily basis. My particular work, exercise and leisure time do not necessitate a sharp outfit. I dress up socially and professionally, so I try to do it well. If my clothes ever get stolen or destroyed, I would just replace them. It's not the end of the world. These things are just things and none of them are irreplaceable. I enjoy certain things because I *enjoy* their functionality - not because I enjoy *having* them. I own a proportionately modest home and motor vehicle. I don't need a high-priced automobile and I have never really wanted one. It's supposed to get me from A to B. I'm not trying to impress anyone. The fact that it does exactly what I need it to do is far more important than the fact that I *own* it. We are taught to judge based on the perception of ownership from a very early age. Our culture is critical of appearances, which can be very deceptive; i.e. most materialistic people basically live on credit – or check-to-check. That's why they seem so destitute when their income stream dries up. It doesn't matter how much you earn if you spend more than you make or save. Cats who flex don't impress me. They make me laugh. I have a 200 dollar cashmere sweater that I bought on clearance, off the rack for 25 dollars. My flyest sweater of all time only cost me a bag of fast food.

It doesn't make any difference to me who knows how much I paid for things. I'm not here to show off, nor am I here to teach you how to shop and consume. If you're not good at shopping, you should probably do less of it. Although I am a great comparison shopper, I do not enjoy it at all. Other than errands for necessities, I only shop a couple of times a year. My lady friends say that a dislike of shopping is just a "guy" thing. But I don't really fit the "guy" mold either. I have no desire for pointless leisure. I have a study – not a man cave. Some women, who can't tell a guy from a man, consider me a "metro" because of my fly nightlife and social occasion style. Ironically, most people in the arts and entertainment industry label me a modern beatnik, which is a stripped-down minimalist version of hepcat style. People who don't like me straight-away mistakenly label me a "hipster"; a term that is widely misused because most people really don't understand the concept of minimalism. In addition, most people don't, won't or can't read, so I don't particularly value public opinion. Someone once asked me if there was such a thing as a "high maintenance minimalist". The answer is yes. All minimalists are high maintenance, because we like what we like and get what we get by all means. I will freely admit that it is sometimes difficult to not be a jerk about it. I often explain that a "starving artist" isn't physically starving but instead puts all their resources into their art; which doesn't leave time and resources for "guy stuff" (which in my mind involves a sofa in some capacity). If you love what you do, then doing it isn't really considered work, therefore excess leisure is neither desired nor necessary. Any dude can be a guy. My goal was to be a man. Manhood is important to me. It has played a vital role in my personal development. After creating this paradigm of what I thought I would be as a man, I am now obligated to my "self" to play the part – or recreate it based on an updated paradigm. I understand now that I created my idealistic self-model because I was in a hurry to grow up. My childhood was not miserable, but I wanted to control my environment.

When our environment is under control, we can more easily relate to it. A key component in understanding all my social default settings is my apparent lack of public self-consciousness. I seem only to be self-conscious when I am alone. I know that doesn't make a lot of sense, but I am my own worst critic. I always have an idealistic image of myself in my mind. I don't see this as strive for perfection. Nothing is perfect. But likewise, nothing is imperfect. Essence and appearance are subjective in perception but objective in reality. I realize that my self-image is not society's view of perfection and I can appreciate that. More than appreciate, actually, I depend on it. My social behavior is a product of subconscious self-reflection and a rejection of "normality". When I am in my element, comfortable and relaxed, everyone and everything is a projection of my imagination. People in my environment only exist because of my interaction with them; and I do not care at all about what is happening or is being said outside the scope of my control. This creates a relaxed atmosphere allowing me to freely interact in any situation. However, when I am far removed from my element, I am constantly removing myself from my "self". Although essence and appearance are partially subjective, I generally obscure my character around those with whom I am not comfortable or in an unwelcome environment. In such an instance, the essence is not a manifestation of all the elements of an object or being (which makes up the appearance) because the reality is incomplete. This incompletion defines me. My demeanor is the envy of honorable men. I attribute this to controlling - rather than being controlled by emotion. I harbor a general sense of melancholy in relation to what we now call "personal development" because I never wanted to develop as a "person". I always thought it would include a lot of bullshit required to interact socially, with no other practical use. At the same time, "human development" seems to be restricted to basic psychology and life sciences as far as modern society is concerned, but that is the type of development I always wanted.

I worried about things way too much as a child.
I was a childhood insomniac. Some nights, I only slept a couple of hours, some nights I did not sleep at all. On the plus side, I wasn't really visibly nervous or anxious about it. My worrying was very adult-like, with little outward sign of distress. I remember being concerned about not sleeping, but I wasn't interested in what was causing it. I had conditioned myself to worry about a lack of sleep, but not enough to do anything about it. Children should never really have to worry about anything, as they live very much in the moment. But for some reason I kept overthinking it, worrying constantly. Until one day, all the sudden I didn't anymore. I can't explain it. I just stopped worrying out of the blue and I never worried again. Nowadays, I rarely let things bother me in any sense. For a while, in my 30's I thought I had become some kind of hill-climbing bohemian or a transcendental Kung-Fu hitch-hiker.

I care about my immediate environment and related elements of my psyche, but I don't worry too much about them. Everything has (or will find) its place. Even when I express concern, it doesn't particularly involve any emotion. I believe this comes from the discovery of purpose, which led to self-awakening and self-awareness. In any case I'm not worried about it. I just accept it for what it is. My Grandmother taught me many things about life. She taught me not to worry about things I could do nothing about. I took that to heart. Then I took it a step further. I feel that legitimate concern may be expressed within the scope of daily routine through centering and balance. Excessive worrying leads to stress, fear, anger and depression. Throw off that yoke and stop pulling the fascist corporate plow. It's systemic servitude. It's psychological slavery and spiritual death. The earth will be here long after you and I are long gone. You cannot "change" the world, you can only change yourself. The world is a construct. Change things about yourself by making better decisions. Develop strong convictions without negative self consciousness or compromised integrity. These elements are within your control.

Yet there will always be something you cannot control. There are variables in life. If you still believe in good and bad, then you will eventually learn to accept that "bad" things happen to "good" people. [the quotations are not relativist, but they are contextual] Everything that occurs in life is part of a larger plan. There are times when we have to let go of all the things we are dragging around emotionally. Especially things related to fear, which can easily control our behavior, and eventually lead to hate. There is no positive benefit to hate, yet hate and fear are the strongest human emotions. While fear and anger are simple paths to hatred, the path of judgment to hatred is a little more complex. Judgment is a major part of human development and may also be the most misunderstood. Prejudgment, for example is a human instinct we all posses. It should always be kept on an individual basis on a corporeal level, which is a difficult standard to follow. Instead, we often judge based on preconceived notions born of social conditioning. We draw conclusions about people based on our recollection of events or situations, either real or imagined, rather than of the moment or in context. Regularly passing judgment based on said notions places us at a disadvantage personally but is socially advantageous, because it's a part of the social formula: we judge, we fear, we hate - and then we consume. It's the system at work. Post-judgment has become socially acceptable because we are also encouraged to be continually offended, by those who can't control their emotions, so they seek to control *yours*. I am amazed at how people are so easily offended by racial slurs and socially incorrect comments and behavior. They're just words. They only have as much meaning as you give them. When I hear an ethnic slur (apart from comedy, of course) I automatically feel superior to the moron who utters it. If I were to become offended, that would only empower that person over me. It lets them know that their words can affect me. I'm not going to let anyone get to me in that sense. The fact that you're even *trying* to get to me, for whatever reason, means that I am automatically better than you.

Most folk nowadays not only allow others to upset them, they practically welcome it. It's almost as if most people want to be offended – just so they can react. I am convinced that most Americans in particular are addicted to emotion, especially so-called personal drama. I remember being highly agitated by most people when I was younger, because I have a rare personality trait called honesty. My parents taught me that in most cases, being honest wasn't "nice". One of my heroes who passed away recently, Patrice O'Neil once said, "It's sad that the word brutal is associated with truth and honesty in our society instead of lies and deceit". We are conditioned to think that the truth is always bad so therefore we should never accept it. But keep in mind, honesty and truth have subjective elements - and some are statistical anomalies. At times, objective or duel truth marks us as a social pariah. We have been so geared toward lying to each other and ourselves, that speaking the truth is automatically villainous. We are raised to be intentionally ignorant and overly sensitive. A common practice is to hate those who speak the truth even more than the truth itself. For those who value truth above all else, it's important not to be dissuaded. No one's opinion is as important as you think. When people react violently or dramatically to the truth, standing firm on that truth is your best defense. Situations that arise from the rejection of truth can be confronted with open-minded self awareness. People often get angry because they realize the truth, but refuse to accept it. Or they just enjoy the drama. If they were confident in their rejection, they wouldn't be angry. But the anger completes their reality. The conscious effort is perpetuated by our sociological systems to maintain a "completeness" of reality for every person, which eliminates the paradox of person vs. human being and discourages any search for truth. In his book *Being and Nothingness*, J.P. Sartre describes man as a creature haunted by a vision of "completion," something Sartre calls the "ens causa sui". Sartre believed that human existence is a conundrum; whereby each of us is in a life-long circuit of nothingness, or free consciousness.

But we are compelled into choice and therefore anguish, as choice (or subjectivity) represents a limit against the scope of our thoughts. However, the fact that we may never understand life's meaning may be meaning in and of itself. In the end, our choices represent failed flights from the anguish of intellectual freedom - to a conditioned, physical world where action is *required*. But such failed dreams of completion, as Sartre described them, inevitably fail to bridge the dichotomy between thought and action, between being and nothingness inherent in our "self". The Buddha proclaimed that suffering is the path to enlightenment. It is becoming more and more apparent to me that we do not suffer in order to obtain enlightenment as a matter of course, but instead we do so for the sake of our inherent desire to be free of the system. We have become systemically contemptuous of God (or lack thereof). We are angry for being born into servitude and we are frustrated at the systems of control for tearing us away from our human self. Nature and self are one - and there should never be a distinction between them. Remember, everything has two sides, including the self. The flip side of self is something I call the "chaos". Either you are in complete control of it - or it is in complete control of you. We will get into that some other time.

As for now, the symbiosis of nature and self is concurrently keeping me grounded and guiding my spirit. This feeling is substantiated by trees swaying in the wind, the earth below and the sun in the sky. I typically use aloe for sunscreen, but the "fruits of nature" so to speak, are often inconvenient on the go. I read that the aloe plant is extinct in the wild and therefore must be farmed instead of gathered, but I don't really believe that. It sounds like a marketing ploy from the naturally-sourced aloe vera gel cultivation folk. Speaking of fruit…"Do y'all have fruit punch?" I ask, yet again, because I legitimately can't remember. "I don't think so", a nice young lady replied politely, while standing behind a counter. I gaze up at a luminous plastic menu trying to decide on a lesser evil - instead of just walking out in support of the greater good.

It isn't what it isn't, I say to myself as I realize that I should be drinking water anyway. So...wait...how long have I been standing here? I don't even remember how I got here. Was I just here a minute ago? Or was that yesterday, or last year, or 2 years ago? It's possible that I never left. It's possible that have been standing here this whole time.

It's possible that all my thoughts occurred in the blink of an eye. It's possible that I only exist in a metaphoric sense. It's possible that I do not exist – and I am merely a figment of your imagination. It's possible that you do not exist – and you are merely a figment of *my* imagination.

The world is an interactive software simulation. The world is a series of shadows on the wall of Plato's cave. The world is a projection on a movie screen. Movies are dreams. Dreams are unconscious preparation for reality. Reality does not exist until it is measured by conscious perception. There is no such thing as nothing. There is no such thing as everything.

All that I am is codependent on all that I am not.
All that I was continually fights against all that I have become -
for possession of my soul. It is the reason I am here.
It is who I am. But it is not *what* I am.
I am "me", I am also my "self" - and I am "I".

And "I don't want to have I go against I",
Bad Brains - I against I, 1986. That song totally kicks.
I finally understand the lyrics, better late than never.

For now "I and I" have complete consciousness; and also perhaps - Enlightenment, suffering, fast food; these things seem to be related in some way.

FIN

www.ingramcontent.com/pod-product-compliance
Lightning Source LLC
Chambersburg PA
CBHW060510030426
42337CB00015B/1826